FRED SCHWED'S

WHERE
ARE THE
CUSTOMERS'
YACHTS?

FRED SCHWED'S

WHERE ARE THE CUSTOMERS' YACHTS?

A MODERN-DAY INTERPRETATION
OF AN INVESTMENT CLASSIC
BY LEO GOUGH

First published in 2010 by
Infinite Ideas Limited
36 St Giles
Oxford, OX1 3LD
United Kingdom
www.infideas.com

A CIP catalogue record for this book is available from the British Library

ISBN 978–1–906821–33–3

Designed and typeset by Cylinder

BRILLIANT IDEAS

INTRODUCTION

In 1940 Fred Schwed, a stockbroker whose father had lost everything as a short seller on Wall Street during the Roaring Twenties, published this timeless classic on how the stock market really works. Schwed, a pleasure-loving, cultured man who had been expelled from Princeton University in his final year for entertaining a lady in his room after 6pm, had a deep understanding and few illusions about the world of investment. He had seen the ups of the 1920s boom and the downs of the 1930s Depression, and his insight into the psychology of investment professionals and their customers is as relevant today, in the current financial crisis, as it was in 1940.

The title of his book, *Where are the Customers' Yachts?*, refers to an old joke: a tourist is being shown all the fancy boats in the harbour, and is told, 'These are the bankers' yachts, and these are the stockbrokers' yachts.' When he asks, innocently, 'Where are the customers' yachts?' he is told that there aren't any (in other words, the customers have not got rich from the stock market).

Schwed is very far from being a cynic, however. He is not saying that investment is pointless, or that private investors never make any money. Rather, he is casting doubt on the ability of the financial services industry to provide any really valuable advice to its customers.

In recent decades great strides have been made in the theoretical understanding of financial markets, but Schwed's wisdom, developed long before the days of hedge funds and exotic derivatives, still holds true. There's a humorous gem on almost every page that strikes a very familiar chord, from the story of the highly paid economist who lugs huge briefcases full of documents to conferences (but never opens them), to the gentle dig at the tendency of analysts to 'develop a prose style which would make a nineteenth century German metaphysician envious'.

Fred Schwed had 'a sneaking fondness for that wretched old hag, the capitalistic system'; in his view, it's much better than the alternatives. His central point is that markets are unpredictable. That doesn't matter if you're investing for the long haul, because all the major stock markets perform well in the long term – it's trying to do better than average, says Schwed, that causes all the trouble.

The follies, the frauds, the fads and the scandals of today are remarkably similar to the ones in Fred Schwed's day. That shouldn't come as a huge surprise, when you read the way that this charming, sophisticated writer deals with the issues of the 1930s and 40s, the truth of the axiom that people never seem to change really hits home. As Michael Lewis says in his foreword to the 1995 edition, 'I like to think that when I first stumbled across this delightful little book the ghost of its author stumbled right along with me, with a gin and tonic in his hand.' Reading Schwed's book is like meeting a friend, and it's a great feeling to realise that not everyone in the markets, then or now, is a money-obsessed barbarian.

1 INCREASING YOUR SAVINGS INCOME – THE WRONG WAY

'Suppose that a family has $100,000 invested in conservative bonds, yielding $3,000 a year: … perhaps the time comes when the family feels they can no longer hold their heads up … unless little Paula goes to a fashionable finishing school. For that it will be necessary to jack up their income yield to $5,500 … Their investment man … can arrange the larger yield in a jiffy … He simply sells out the conservative bonds and substitutes riskier securities.'

Fred Schwed goes on to point out that what Paula learns at finishing school may turn out to be all she has to face life with, if the family's capital is lost in the riskier securities.

DEFINING IDEA...
Distrust and caution are the parents of security.
~ BENJAMIN FRANKLIN

These days, the people who try to live on their investment income are generally already retired. Anyone who can work is usually advised to reinvest their investment income, and not to spend it. This is sensible advice, and it applies to able-bodied retired people too. If you don't have to spend your investment income, don't do it! By adding it to your capital, you will help it to grow, which will potentially give you a larger investment income in the future.

What is really fatal is to try to increase your income by putting your nest egg in riskier investments. British government bonds, for instance, are less risky than, say, Indonesian government bonds. Even before the current financial crisis, it was clear that the high street banks in Britain were likely to be a safer place to deposit money than, say, Icelandic banks, because Britain is a larger and stronger economy than Iceland. The market is aware of these differences in risk. That's why Indonesian bonds offer a better return than UK government bonds, and why Icelandic banks were offering a better interest rate to depositors than British banks did before the crisis of 2008.

Most of the time, if there are two similar investments and one offers a better return than the other, it is because it is a riskier investment. No one really knows exactly how much riskier it is, of course, but if you are trying to keep your capital as safe as possible so that it can go on paying out an income for many years into the future, don't increase your risk, and DON'T move your capital into riskier investments!

HERE'S AN IDEA FOR YOU...

At the time of writing, interest rates are lower than they have been for generations. The pundits keep telling us that this is good news for borrowers and bad news for savers. If you are living on your investment income, though, you will have been enduring low fixed income rates for many years already. Yes, they are even lower now, but don't succumb to the temptation of investing in riskier things in order to increase your income. Look for other ways of coping, such as: tightening your belt, getting a part-time job, or selling a few things you have in the house. Interest rates will go up eventually – your objective must be to preserve your capital, and the best way to do that is to keep it in the safest assets you can find, even though they don't pay the best rates.

2 SPECULATION

'Speculation is an effort, probably unsuccessful, to turn a little money into a lot.'

DEFINING IDEA...

There are two times in a man's life when he should not speculate: when he can't afford it, and when he can.

~ MARK TWAIN

Much is made of the difference between investment (a 'sensible' activity) and speculation (a 'risky' activity) but, as Schwed points out, it is not always easy to tell the difference between the two. Plenty of cautious investors have lost money in what they thought were safe investments, sometimes through skulduggery but more often because the investments turned out not to be quite as safe as all the experts thought they were. So you might say that investments that were generally thought to be safe but actually resulted in losses should be classed in the speculative category. This doesn't help us much though, because as investors we need a definition that can help us make decisions about the future; just saying that all past loss-makers were speculative doesn't tell us anything useful.

To understand speculation, you need to understand human nature. It is very natural and human to get excited and confident when you have made some money easily and it looks as if you are going to make a lot more even more easily – that's how the psychology of booms works, when even normally cautious people start plunging into riskier and riskier investments. But real speculators, the people who are just naturally inclined to take large risks, are different: they will speculate whatever the market is doing, whether it is going up, down or sideways.

Beginners at stock market investment often try their hands at speculation. This is unwise, because they don't understand the market very well. Typically, beginners think, 'If I can pick a few winning shares, I can sell out when the price goes up and make a quick profit.' The odds are against them, for two main reasons. First, there is very good evidence that no one, even the experts, is much good at picking winning shares consistently. The famous exceptions to this rule, such as Warren Buffett, are discussed in chapter 37 (basically, they improve their odds using methods that are not available to the ordinary investor). Second, most beginner investors have no idea how to evaluate a particular company or to assess the risks of a given investment.

Is speculation always foolish, and will it always end in tears? Not necessarily. For example, if you have better knowledge than others about a particular investment or situation, you may judge that it is less risky than other people realise. As a speculator, you look for opportunities where there is a high reward to risk ratio; if you can find them, you'll make money. In the major stock markets, however, such opportunities are rare – to find them, you'll have to go further afield, to developing countries or outside the stock market altogether.

HERE'S AN IDEA FOR YOU...

The stock market is a game that is designed to foil speculation. If you really want to take large risks and be able to influence the outcome of your investment, you would be wiser to try your hand at a real business; if you choose the right business and run it well, your chances of making large profits are generally better than if you speculate in the stock market.

3 SHARE PRICES DON'T ALWAYS GO UP

'[The SEC] not only want an orderly market, but a market that shall forever gently rise. Of course, that conception is just plain silly, like Voltaire's suggestion that a community ought to be able to support itself by everybody taking in everybody else's washing.'

To someone new to the stock market, it might seem quite a good idea for the government to make sure that share prices always go up. It could pass laws to that effect. Then it could make the regulatory body – in the US, this is the SEC (Securities and Exchange Commission) and in the UK, it is the FSA (Financial Services Authority) – force the market to nudge up share prices by a small fraction, say once a month. After all, wouldn't most investors be happy with a small profit every month?

DEFINING IDEA...

It is difference of opinion that makes horse races.

– MARK TWAIN

The idea is completely unworkable, of course, and the regulators know it. What Schwed is complaining about here is that regulators are pressurised, especially in times of crisis, to make pious and reassuring statements about the market to the public. Today the public is more knowledgeable about investment than it was in Schwed's day, but not by much; it is still extremely poorly informed about the stock market and economics in general, and it wants to be told that the government will make everything all right. But that's not how markets work.

To be attractive to investors, a stock market depends upon its ability to allow investors to buy and sell shares at any time when the market is open. On large stock exchanges, like London and New York, millions of shares exchange hands every day, and the share prices are always changing (usually by only a tiny fraction). But in order to sell your shares, there has to be a buyer, and if a government stepped in to force prices up artificially, there would come a point when there would be no buyers: the price would be too high. People would start looking for other ways to invest and billions would drain out of the market and go overseas to other stock exchanges.

To function properly, a stock market has to allow prices to fall as well as rise. That's what investors really want. If Megaboom Plc loses billions and comes near to bankruptcy, you would want to see those losses reflected in its share price, wouldn't you? If you wouldn't, then don't become a stock market investor!

But why would anyone sensible buy Megaboom's shares if they dropped? Simple: it's because they think that the shares have gone down too far, and that Megaboom's business will recover. That's a matter of opinion – and that's what drives the market.

HERE'S AN IDEA FOR YOU...

In the long term, on average, share prices in the world's stock markets do rise, and at a better rate than other kinds of financial assets, such as bonds or cash deposits. To take advantage of this, most experienced investors put a lot of their money into carefully selected unit trusts and investment trusts. If you decide to do this, make yourself this promise: you won't touch the money for a minimum of five years. This will increase your odds of a satisfactory outcome.

4 THE FUTURE OF INVESTMENT

'Investment is an effort, which should be successful, to prevent a lot of money from becoming a little.'

Usually we think of investment as a way of making our money grow. So what does Schwed mean by saying it's really a way of protecting our money from shrinking?

DEFINING IDEA...
Castles made of sand slip into the sea eventually
– JIMI HENDRIX, MUSICIAN

To understand this, think about a very long period of time – say 2,000 years. Do you think it would be possible to grow your wealth consistently and pass it on to your descendants for such a long period of time? It has probably never been done, although some people, like the Norman nobles, did try to preserve their wealth by passing it on to the first son in each generation. It doesn't work. First, your direct line may die out. If your direct line of descendants doesn't die out, you would probably have so many descendants that the wealth would get diluted (this happened to the wealthy Vanderbilt family in less than 150 years). Furthermore, the structures that allow safe investment – like nation states, property laws, banking systems and so on – don't last that long. Over the last 2,000 years there have been many times when violent political change has caused the wealthy to lose everything – think of Genghis Khan's invasions, or the Russian Revolution.

If that doesn't convince you that wealth cannot be kept indefinitely, consider this: if you had been able to deposit, say, £10,000 in a bank at 5% interest in the year 1 AD (which you couldn't have, because there weren't any banks), compound interest would have built your deposit up so that it would now be worth more than all the money in the world.

All this may sound ridiculous, but there is a serious point: investment, as we think of it today, has only really existed since the nineteenth century. In our own time we have seen a great democratisation of investment, as more and more people have gained access to the money economy, bank accounts, the stock market, and so on. Our investment survival depends upon the financial system remaining stable in the future. Yes, the system may well outlive us, but can we really be sure it will be there in 300 years' time, say?

This insight should inform our strategy. Knowing that we cannot build up wealth that will last for centuries, we should focus on building up enough to keep ourselves in our old age and a sum that we can pass on to our children to give them a start in life. If we are lucky enough to have attained that much wealth early in life, it will be a full time job to preserve it. That's because society has a way of chipping away at large fortunes until there is nothing left. Remember all those Edwardian gentlemen of leisure, who didn't have to work for a living? Most of their descendants have had to get regular jobs.

HERE'S AN IDEA FOR YOU...

You may not be able to pass your wealth on to your descendants in 4010, but you can pass it on to your children. Make a will – and appoint trusted friends, not lawyers or bankers, as executors. That way, you'll keep expensive professional fees to a minimum.

5 BOOMS GO 'BOOM'!

'In our moment of sober thought we all realize that booms are bad things, not good. But nearly all of us have a secret hankering for another one.'

Fred Schwed lived through the Roaring Twenties, when middle class people in America had a whale of a time, dancing the Charleston, drinking illegal booze, and making easy money as the stock market soared. Then he had to endure the grim days of the Great Crash of 1929 and the years of the Great Depression of the 1930s.

DEFINING IDEA...

We will never return to the old boom and bust.

– GORDON BROWN IN 2007, JUST BEFORE THE 2008 BUST

At the time of writing, we are in the midst of a global financial crisis that has followed a long boom in easy consumer credit. A lot of people are hoping that the boom days will come back soon. It's easy to understand why: when it was easy to borrow large sums, house prices soared in the UK. The higher the house price, the easier it was to release large chunks of spending money by remortgaging. And money was cheap, by historical standards (at the time of writing money is still very cheap in the UK, but this is unlikely to last for long and in any case it is hard to borrow). There are many people who are young enough to have first entered the house market during the boom, and whose only experience, until the present crisis, was of easy money and rising prices. They don't remember the long, miserable periods in the past – like the times when inflation was over 20%, or when almost nobody could get a mortgage, or when young people couldn't get any kind of a job. And even if you are old enough to remember those bad times, you would probably prefer not to.

The fact is, there are good times and bad times in economic life. They are often called cycles, but they are not very regular or predictable cycles. One of the main secrets of economic survival is not to behave as if a boom is going to last forever – they never do. When the crash comes, it's the people who have borrowed too much who get hit the hardest.

Money will probably be tight for a long time. Wages probably won't rise much, and jobs will be hard to find. You won't be getting 15 invitations to get a new credit card dropping through your door every week. The word 'shopaholic' will begin to seem quaint and old-fashioned.

Never mind. It's not the end of the world. Focus on the productive aspects of your life, like building your career, saving, and paying your mortgage, and muddle through; one fine day you'll start to notice another boom beginning. You'll probably make a fool of yourself in that boom, too, but just try to make sure you keep it within sensible limits.

HERE'S AN IDEA FOR YOU...

If you borrow, try to borrow for constructive purposes, like buying somewhere to live, or a car to get you to work, or good clothes that will help you get a good job. That's 'good' debt. 'Bad' debt is when you borrow money at high rates of interest (for example by using store cards or credit cards) and spend it on things you don't need. Pay off those cards!

6 PROFESSIONAL STOCK-PICKING

'Thus far in our history there has been little evidence that there exists a demonstrable skill in managing security portfolios.'

DEFINING IDEA...

I have no confidence in professional stock-picking.

– PROFESSOR ALFRED STEINHERR, EMINENT BANKER

In spite of all the hype, the grand offices, the PhDs in finance, the serried ranks of bright young professionals and the genuine advances in the theoretical understanding of finance and investment during the last half century, it is still as true today as it was in Fred Schwed's that professional managers, as a group, have not demonstrated that they can consistently perform better than the average over an extended period of time (for an explanation of what 'average' may mean see chapter 13).

It should be said though, that professional fund managers in general are probably better at managing security portfolios than you are, at least when dealing with technical matters. They are less likely than the average person to make a silly mistake, like buying the wrong shares, which is easy to do when a company has more than one kind of share in issue, or like invalidating a share application form by filling it in incorrectly. We can reasonably expect them to act 'professionally' in the sense of performing their duties to a good standard. But this is not at all the same as having a special skill in knowing which shares to buy, or when to buy and sell them. No one has the ability to always pick shares whose prices will go up.

This insight has been confirmed by numerous studies of the performance of professionally managed funds. In general, the majority of funds perform worse than the market as a whole, and even the funds that do outperform the market generally are unable to keep it up for many years. There are a few exceptions, of course, but statistically we would expect there to be a few exceptions as the result of chance.

In recent years Americans, who are generally a bit more clued-in about the stock market than we are in Britain, have become rather fed up with this state of affairs. Why should a private investor, they ask, pay for expertise in stock-picking when it is not clear that such an ability really exists? Some market professionals respond vigorously by arguing that some talented people do seem to be very good at stock-picking, at least on the face of it. But there aren't very many of them, and often their funds are rather large and overpriced, so they won't necessarily perform particularly well in the future.

This is the great problem of investment. The really big gains are generally made by a stock-picker who is not very well-known. Once the stock-picker becomes famous everyone watches him or her like a hawk, and the returns tend to go down as competitors start to copy the methods. To be successful, a stock-picking method must be both inherently sound and unpopular.

HERE'S AN IDEA FOR YOU...

Tired of less than exciting fund performance? Why not pick a tracker fund, which simply mimics the performance of a stock market index. It will probably slightly under perform the index, but not by much, and you'll probably do a lot better than most fund managers! You can find tracker funds quoted in the financial press.

7 SPEND YOUR INCOME, NOT YOUR CAPITAL.

'A man's true wealth is his income, not his bank balance. There are times and places when it is better to have a hundred thousand dollars than it was to have had two hundred thousand at another time and place.'

DEFINING IDEA...

A large income is the best recipe for happiness I ever heard of.
– JANE AUSTEN

The main point here is that it is your current income, not your total assets, and especially not your financial assets, that governs your lifestyle and how wealthy you feel. The purchasing power of your money may vary from time to time, but you should try to avoid drawing down capital to spend as if it were income.

Many of us don't have much in the way of assets, so we fail to appreciate this important difference. To someone with no assets, all money looks like spending money. But capital - which means your valuable possessions, like houses, cars and pension funds - is hard to acquire and easy to lose, so it is very important to make the distinction between money you need to keep, and money you can spend.

To understand the difference, consider the following example:

First, let's imagine Fred, a supermarket shelf stacker who wins 5 million quid on the lottery. The first mistake he makes is to tell all his friends and relatives. A lot of them will automatically expect a handout, which will whittle away at his lump sum. Next, he decides to be sensible and buys some houses for himself and his relatives. That's fine, but he probably buys houses that are quite expensive to maintain. Next, he gives up his job - that would be fine if he was going to train to get a better job, but no. He goes off on a series of world cruises with his mates, drinks a lot, and gets into bad spending habits. When he finally gets home, he buys a lot of expensive sports cars. A few years down the line, he's a bored, lazy good-for-nothing. After a while, the champagne lifestyle, the upkeep of the houses and cars, and all the loans he has to make to his fair-weather friends, start to bite. Pretty soon Fred finds that he will have to get a job in order to maintain his lifestyle, but any job he can get probably won't generate enough money. Slowly some of the cars have to go. Then maybe the houses will have to go too. It's an old story, but it happens quite often. It is amazingly easy to get through millions of pounds in only a few years and have little or nothing to show for it at the end.

What Fred should have done, of course, from a financial point of view, is to have said, 'This 5 million quid is capital, not income. I'm going to invest it and live off the income.' At 4%, say, his capital could have given him an income of £200,000 per year for the rest of his life, far more than most people earn or need.

HERE'S AN IDEA FOR YOU...

Next time a lump sum falls into your lap, leap into action and DON'T spend it! Put it away in a bank deposit, bonds or shares, and leave it to grow.

8 CAPITAL MARKETS

'We all have a fondness for articles which can only be produced in plants costing millions of dollars. Few of these articles can be produced by a fellow and his uncle working behind the garage. The only successful method so far devised for getting millions out of the public, for enterprises good and bad, is some system similar to the devious mechanisms of Wall Street.'

DEFINING IDEA...

Capitalism is what people do when you leave them alone.

– KENNETH MINOGUE, POLITICAL SCIENTIST

If you really want to understand the stock market, think about it from a company's point of view. Companies need money in order to function, to make profits, and, especially, to grow bigger. They can get money in three main ways. First, they can reinvest their profits. This is a nice, safe way that is appropriate for some types of business, but its disadvantage is that it severely limits the rate at which the company can grow. If you have a new product that will potentially make a fortune over a period of, say, five years, reinvesting your profits will not enable you to grow fast enough to enable you to take full advantage of your market opportunity. In today's cut-throat business world, you'll be pushed aside by a better financed company and wind up with only a small share of the market. This often happens to small companies.

The second way to get money for growth is to borrow it. This isn't a bad way, but you have to pay interest, and you'll have to convince a bunch of glassy eyed, unimaginative bankers that your project is likely to succeed.

The third way is to raise money by selling shares in your company to investors. The new shareholders become, in effect, sleeping partners in your company, enjoying any increase in the value of the company and also receiving dividend payments that you make out of the profits. If your company is large enough, this can be done by selling shares to the general public through a stock market. It is not an easy or cheap process, but if it is properly done it can raise massive amounts of capital for your enterprise relatively quickly, so it is a great way to finance growth.

This is the basic reason for the existence of the stock markets. It is a way of matching savers, like you and me, with productive organisations, like successful companies.

HERE'S AN IDEA FOR YOU...

The great advantage of the major stock markets is their liquidity. You can sell most shares at any time that the market is open. Compare that with the situation when some friends ask you to buy shares in their small business; you may never be able to sell the shares and get your money back. It is the liquidity, and relative stability, of most publicly traded companies that make stock market investing more attractive than small company investing to most people. In some countries, particularly in the Far East, many people keep large sums of money in the bank permanently so that it remains liquid. This is unwise - they would get a better return in the stock markets. If all your savings are in cash or bonds, think about putting at least some of it in the stock market – it will still be liquid.

9 PROBABILITY

'If a man has tossed a coin 'heads' four times in succession, which do you think he is more likely to toss the fifth time, heads or tails? (If you think he is more likely to toss heads or tails, look into the interior decorating game. You have that instinctive type of mentality which might do very well at that.)'

Most people can read and write, but many people are stunningly innumerate. You cannot hope to do well in the stock market unless you have a grasp of the art and science of large numbers and in particular of mathematical probability.

At school, you tend to learn about probability in your early teens, when you have other things on your mind. It is usually, or at least it was in my day, presented in a very abstract way. Yet the great mathematicians of the seventeenth and eighteenth centuries loved to present their mathematical problems in terms of gambling, which makes them a lot more interesting.

DEFINING IDEA...

The probable is what usually happens.

– ARISTOTLE

And if you think that the stock market is a gamble - which it doesn't have to be - there's all the more reason to get a good grasp of probability. So, do you understand why, if you toss heads four times in a row, it makes no difference to the probable outcome of the fifth toss, assuming that the coin hasn't been doctored and that it is therefore equally likely to fall either way? It's because each toss of the coin is completely unrelated to the next one. The chance remains 50\50 each time. You may get long runs of all heads or all tails, but that is simply the result of chance; it is not a trend. A series of outcomes where the odds have been 50\50 each time constitutes a truly random sequence - there is no hidden pattern to it.

In the short-term, according to many statisticians, share prices tend to approximate this level of randomness. There is really no good reason why a price goes up a tick one minute and down a tick the next minute. There is even a theory, called the Random Walk theory, that attempts to explain much of how share prices change in these terms.

Over longer periods, though, share price movements look a lot less random. Companies that are doing well in the real world, for instance, tend to enjoy substantial rises in their share price as investors become willing to pay higher prices for the shares. The great question is whether the price of a share is fair, a bargain, or expensive. Nobody really knows what the true price should be because this is subject to market forces, which are almost impossible to measure in most real world situations.

HERE'S AN IDEA FOR YOU...

Probability is the ABC of investment. If you don't understand it, you shouldn't be an investor. And it is really not that difficult to understand. Go and get a good textbook on the subject, one that explains things clearly and has good diagrams. Work your way through it, and make sure you understand it. In a few weeks you will have a thorough grounding that will free you to think much more clearly about investments of all kinds.

10 WHO TO BLAME?

'While 'hundreds of thousands are being plunged into poverty' only the thoughtful ask, 'What is happening to us'. The popular cry is 'Who is doing this to us' and its satisfying sequel – 'Just let me get my hands on him!' The public goes raging about like an infuriated mob with a rope.'

When I first read these lines years ago I thought 'We're more sensible these days. The media are more savvy, and even the politicians have a better understanding of finance than they used to.' How wrong I was.

Since the beginning of the financial crisis in 2007 we have been subjected to a procession of almost comically hysterical pronouncements in the highbrow media as well as in the gutter press, that have been just about as wrong as wrong can be. New pundits have shot to fame on their purported ability (virtually invisible) to explain to the public how They (that's the wicked high financiers) have messed everything up. Acquaintances, who have never had any interest in finance or economics, are suddenly up in arms, demanding the imprisonment (and possibly the execution) of those responsible. What's more, everyone seems pretty sure who is to blame.

Well, yes, the bankers were greedy and short-termist and the politicians looked the other way, and the regulators were unbelievably craven, and some academics blew a lot of hot air about how wonderful derivatives were (see chapter 12). But what about us, the general public? During the last ten years or so it became increasingly easy to borrow money – unbelievably so. People could borrow much more than their annual incomes and just spend it on fun things like holidays and designer clothes – they didn't even have to pretend that they were renovating their house in order to get it.

All that money had to come from somewhere. Did you earn it, or did you borrow on the expectation of a better salary or a further increase in the value of your house? It's the same with all booms. Their technical causes may be quite different, but the results always boil down to the same thing – suddenly there isn't any money any more, and the people who borrowed the most get hit the hardest.

So we, the public, have to take part of the blame. If you borrowed more than you could afford, you were as much a part of the problem as those wicked bankers who were selling dodgy mortgages on the wholesale market. When there is a systemic problem, it really isn't the fault of just one group of people, however unsavoury they may be.

HERE'S AN IDEA FOR YOU...

Do yourself a massive favour and limit the amount of time you spend listening to and watching commentary about the stock market and the economy in general. Most of it is incomplete, misleading and worse than useless. Focus on what is important to your overall investment plans, like getting to know one or two industries really well, and being well-informed on key indicators, such as interest rates, unemployment figures and inflation. Knowing where you are is more than half the battle – no one can tell you exactly what the future will bring, so don't waste much time listening to them.

11 POPULAR SHARES

'Those classes of investment considered the 'best' change from period to period. The pathetic fallacy is that what are thought to be the best are in truth only the most popular – the most active, the most talked of, the most boosted, and, consequently, the highest priced at that time.'

Anyone remember the dot.com boom? That was when internet stocks – whatever that meant, and believe me it was often very hard to know what it meant – were the things to buy. You weren't hip, you weren't cool, indeed you were barely a human being if you weren't buying internet stocks and chatting about them to other buyers on the internet. Then it all went 'phut', lots of people lost money, and some people even went to jail.

DEFINING IDEA...
Everything popular is wrong.
– OSCAR WILDE

At the time, though, all kinds of stuffed shirts were pontificating about how the new internet companies were going to overthrow the 'old-fashioned' businesses. There were going to be no more shops, for instance – now there's a notion that has yet to manifest itself in the real world! The point is not that all internet companies were bad, far from it – some of them seem to be doing very well indeed, a decade on. It's that during the dot.com boom internet stocks were very, very popular, and it was very hard to tell the good companies from the bad ones, or even the risky companies from the not so risky.

Fred Schwed is absolutely right. Whatever type of shares are said to be the best at any given moment, they are really only the most popular. Yes, their share prices may have gone up, but that may be only because of their temporary popularity. During the internet boom people were investing in companies that had no profits, and often no income, on incredibly high multiples of their estimated first year's profits. The idea was to get in on the ground floor of some new software or special approach and then make a mint when and if some ageing dinosaur company bought it up for a massive amount. Well, yes, that did happen to a few companies – but it didn't happen to a lot of other firms.

Until you have experienced the irrational nature of a boom in a certain type of investment, you can never fully appreciate it. Surely all these well-educated, shrewd, grossly overpaid, people know what they are talking about? During boom times, a lot them don't – they get as foolishly enthusiastic as the rest of the lemmings. And there are others who just take advantage of a boom by trying to make customers feel as if they are stupid if they don't get in on the action – so be cautious.

HERE'S AN IDEA FOR YOU...

Innovations are wonderful things. Improvements in transport, medicine, agriculture and communications have transformed our world utterly over the last 200 years or so. But that doesn't mean that investing in innovations, even ones that are of huge benefit to mankind, necessarily works out well for the investors. For example, many investors lost fortunes in the canals, the railways and the internet. So next time a wonderful new industry appears that promises to change the world, take a long, hard look at it before you decide to invest.

12 DERIVATIVES

'Option brokers are fond of pointing out all the advantageous ways there are of 'operating once an option gets into the money'. It is indeed the truth; one can do more fascinating things with an option than an inventive boy can do with a set of Meccano. But for some subtle reason, whatever one does at this point usually turns out to be wrong.'

Derivatives have existed for hundreds of years, but in Fred Schwed's day they were limited to only a few types, such as 'options', which allow you to speculate on the option to buy or sell a share at an agreed price at a fixed future date, by which time you hope that the market price has moved in your favour.

DEFINING IDEA...
Derivatives are financial weapons of mass destruction.
– WARREN BUFFETT

Since the 1990s, however, derivatives have mushroomed. You can now gamble on a huge range of financial derivatives. The future prices of almost anything, from stock indexes to soya beans, are available, and you can construct fantastically complex bets with them. This has come about because of a number of mathematical discoveries, most notably the Black Scholes model, for which its discoverers won a Nobel Prize, which enabled more accurate pricing of these exotic products.

The most important thing you should know about derivatives is that they do not represent 'real' financial assets that you own. They are contracts – i.e. promises – that are 'derived' from real assets, indices or events. And promises can be broken. When Long Term Capital Management, one of the first firms to use derivatives on a massive scale, got into trouble, there was a serious danger of global financial meltdown if it reneged on the derivatives contracts it had taken out. A consortium of major banks had to step in to prop up the firm for long enough for it to 'unwind' its positions.

So, derivatives are intrinsically dangerous because their market is potentially worth many times more than the actual value of the 'real' assets upon which they are based. One eminent banker, Alfred Steinherr, has called them the 'wild beast of finance'.

But if they are so dangerous, why are they so popular, and why are so many bright young sparks training to become derivatives experts? Well, part of the answer lies in the increased competition in the financial markets. Large banks, for example, have seen their profit margins squeezed in many of their traditional banking activities. To keep their profits up, they have entered the derivatives markets, for example by offering to arrange complex 'hedges' for their customers. A true 'hedge', in the sense of hedging your bets, is where you place a number of bets in such a way that you will not lose whatever the outcome. The trouble is, most derivatives transactions are not true hedges; sometimes the outcome is that you unexpectedly wind up with a massive loss.

HERE'S AN IDEA FOR YOU...

If you really can't resist a flutter, do it in a disciplined way. Set aside a sum of money – preferably a small percentage of your total financial assets – and keep it in a separate account. Use it to experiment in derivatives to your heart's content, until it is all gone.

13 STOCK INDICES

'Of course, in any of these complex matters, if we could be sure we had all the figures, plus all the pertinent footnotes, which to a greater extent invalidate most of the figures, then we would certainly have something, even if it were only the blind staggers.'

DEFINING IDEA...

We must never make average descriptions of experiments, because the true relations of phenomena disappear in the average.

– CLAUDE BERNARD, NINETEENTH-CENTURY SCIENTIST

Good performance in the stock market, we are told, means 'above-average performance'. This sounds reasonable enough, until we start to investigate what 'average' really means. It is actually quite hard to find out. For example, there isn't a page in the *Financial Times* that tells you in plain language that the stock market's average performance over the last 12 months was X. What you can find in the financial press, however, are figures for stock market indices, such as the FTSE 100, the FTSE 350, the NYSE, the NASDAQ and so on. Indices aren't strictly speaking averages, but they are about as close as we can get. In recent years new indices have been created, such as Morgan Stanley's MSCI series, which provide useful information by which to compare and judge the performance of more exotic financial arenas, such as the emerging markets in Asia, South America and Africa.

These indices are definitely better than nothing, but they can give a false impression of precision in a very complex world where surprisingly little can be measured precisely. For a start, indices are not really 'averages' as we would normally understand the term. They are usually, but not always, based on collections of shares that have something in common, such as all being in the biotechnology business, or being the biggest companies by market capitalisation in a particular country. Market capitalisation, by the way, is the number you get if you add up the market value of all the shares of a company currently in issue. Indices are not all constructed in the same way, and most of them are 'weighted' according to various arcane criteria in order to make them more representative.

Some indices don't seem to be particularly representative of anything. The Dow Jones Industrial Average (DJIA), for example, the world's second oldest index which was started in the 1890s, is often thought to represent American industry as a whole, but it really doesn't. Currently the DJIA consists of only 30 large companies, and is price weighted, which means higher priced shares count for much more than lower priced shares, irrespective of the actual size of the company.

As investors, we should really care about the long term performance of our portfolios and not the short-term ups and downs. Suppose you were to check your portfolio after 15 years and found that it had outperformed the index; then you could crow about 'beating the averages'!

HERE'S AN IDEA FOR YOU...

If you are thinking of investing in a unit trust or an investment trust, always read the prospectus carefully. The trust should tell you by what benchmark it should be measured. This benchmark is usually an index, and is meant to be representative of the kinds of industries or firms that the trust invests in. The fund manager hopes to outperform the index. So if the fund doesn't outperform the index consistently the manager has some explaining to do.

14 THE TROUBLE WITH ACCOUNTING

'A not implausible argument could be presented to show that accounting is not even an art, but just a state of mind.'

DEFINING IDEA...

If you get interested in a company and you read the annual report ... you will have done more than 98% of the people on Wall Street.

~ JIM ROGERS, INVESTMENT GURU

Accounts are not what they appear to be. For example, it is very difficult indeed to compare the accounts of two different companies meaningfully in any detail. The categories they use, and the things they put in those categories, tend to be quite different. And when it comes to comparing company accounts from different countries, the task becomes well-nigh impossible. Different employment laws, different tax regimes, different terminology and different accounting practices mean that when you try to compare the accounts of, say, a fruit company in Brazil with another one based in Germany (which has subsidiaries in five other countries on three continents) you will struggle to discover anything meaningful.

The problem with accounting is not so much that people are dishonest (although some are) but that you really need to have a lot of accounting knowledge to be able to interpret accounts correctly. This task is made harder because publicly traded firms are not required to reveal everything about themselves to the public in their annual reports. This is reasonable, because some accounting information is commercially sensitive (it might help their competitors, for instance).

Professional investment firms employ legions of specialists, known as 'share analysts' to trawl through company accounts and compare them with what else they can find out about the firms and their industries. Some theorists believe that in the major markets, like the US and the UK, so many analysts are at work that their insights in effect, cancel each other out, and make the current market price the 'fair price', given the available knowledge about the company at that time. However, it is very clear that this cannot be the case in the less active stock markets around the world, where often very few people know much about the companies listed there. The trouble is that the annual reports of firms in such markets are often not very reliable either, but intrepid investors sometimes try to make a killing by searching out the hidden gems buried away in obscure markets.

One acquaintance of mine made a fortune by investing in a brewery in Mongolia just after the collapse of communism. The accounts weren't worth a damn, he said, but he could tell from the cash flow statement that more money was coming in than was going out, and he took a bet that with Mongolia opening up to commerce, more people would be buying the local beer. It took a few years, but eventually his gamble paid off.

HERE'S AN IDEA FOR YOU...

When you get hold of a company's annual report, start reading it from the back – that's what the pros do. They're looking for all the little secrets that are buried away in the notes to the accounts. These can sometimes be very important – for example, 'Oh and by the way we have a £100 million lawsuit against us which, if we lose, could wipe out our entire profits for the year'.

15 NO MOMENTUM IN PRICES

'The stock market … not being a physical thing, is not subject to Newton's laws of propulsion or inertia.'

DEFINING IDEA...

Blinded by greed and wishful thinking we often seem to believe that huge and growing market momentum is a strong signal that a pattern will continue. In fact, such momentum often creates the very conditions that produce a painful correction.

– DAVID ROWE, EXECUTIVE VICE PRESIDENT, SUNGUARD

This is one of the hardest things about the stock market to understand, which is why financial writers return to the point again and again. It's even in the 'wealth warnings' on investment literature, where they tell you that 'the past movements of share prices are not necessarily a guide' to future movements. They're right! In spades! But this is hard to grasp because we are used to a physical world in which objects obey physical forces. When we see a ball rolling down a hill, for instance, we can make a pretty good guess at the path it will travel. The stock market isn't like that at all. It isn't driven by physical laws in the same way as a ball, but even experienced investors often forget this, and start unconsciously to use a physical model in order to estimate where it is going to go next.

Stock market jargon is full of expressions that suggest that prices are subject to physical laws. One of the current hot terms is 'traction'. Exciting new companies, especially in technology, are often said to have 'traction', which means that they are supposed to have a bright future of rising share prices, impelled by some real yet invisible force.

Well, yes and no. The real and invisible force that moves share prices is of course the net effect of many transactions made by investors large and small, in other words, it is the result of decisions made by many different people. Investors don't always sell because they think a share price is going to drop; a large fund, for instance, might decide to sell off its holdings in a particular firm because of a policy change or a strategic decision that has nothing to do with the performance of that particular share. And if investor excitement is supposed to be the force behind 'traction', then we have to say that it is a pretty fickle thing. Betting on other investors' enthusiasm for a share is a bit like playing musical chairs: you hope that you will be one of the ones who finds a chair (i.e. sells before the price drops) when the music stops.

Many, many investors play musical chairs, but they would be better off if they found a firm that went from strength to strength in the long term and just ignored the temporary ups and downs.

HERE'S AN IDEA FOR YOU...

When you invest, invest to a plan. Have a review once or twice a year at a regular time and adjust your portfolio, and the rest of the time, leave it alone. Don't check your share prices, and don't watch the financial channels on satellite. Stick to your plan for long enough – say five or ten years – to be able to judge whether it has worked. Constant buying and selling is murderous to your profits!

16 TECHNICAL ANALYSIS

'This writer does not believe that [chartists] can predict the future with any accuracy.'

Technical analysis (TA), or charting, is an old stock market practice that began long before more scientific approaches, such as share analysis, which became professionalised during the 1930s. The appeal of TA is to the false instinct that we all seem to have that share prices are somehow predictable because they seem to follow physical laws.

DEFINING IDEA...

Never make forecasts, especially about the future.

– SAM GOLDWYN, MOVIE PRODUCER

There are many kinds of chartists and charting methods; for example, some try to identify Fibonacci numbers in price movements. Fibonacci numbers were discovered in the thirteenth century by an Italian mathematician of the same name, and sometimes occur in nature – for example in the spirals of florets on a sunflower. Each number is the sum of the previous two numbers, starting with 0 and 1. The sequence begins 0, 1, 1, 2, 3, 5, 8, 13, 21, 34, and goes on to infinity. Another popular TA method is to look for patterns that repeat themselves; for example, a small peak, followed by a larger one, followed by a smaller one is called a 'head and shoulders' and is supposed to be followed by a large drop.

Charting doesn't really work, or at least, not well enough for people to make money out of it. It's no good arguing with chartists – you can no more change their minds than you can that of a member of an extreme religious cult. If they lose a lot of money, which they often do, because charting encourages you to trade too often, they tend to explain it by saying that they didn't follow their own rules closely enough.

Chartism doesn't work because, essentially, it is looking for patterns that aren't really there. The human brain, which evolved when we were struggling for existence in a hostile natural environment, is designed to look for patterns everywhere. Seeing patterns in little flickers of light, or sudden changes in temperature, might have been very useful in helping us to find things to eat, back in the Stone Age, but it doesn't help us to predict the future of share prices today. This pattern-seeking quality leads to 'over-fitting' complex data into seemingly reliable patterns that, a long time later, turn out not to have been the patterns we thought they were.

On the 'sell side' of the financial services industry, which are those units that exist to sell financial products and services, there is a natural tendency to tell people what they want to hear. And if some people want TA advice, that's what they will get, as long as it remains a legal, if preposterous, theory.

HERE'S AN IDEA FOR YOU...

Do you think it would be reasonable to speculate on share prices by taking the advice of an astrologer? A lot of people in the Far East do this, and the major banks even offer such advice as part of their service (not in so many words of course, but when you're alone in a room with a bank representative, you can get some astrological advice if you ask for it). Why not try running two portfolios, one based on TA and one on astrology, and see which one does better?

17 GOOD STORIES

'It is hard to sell Americans a propositon that hasn't the promise of a little zip in it.'

America's experience over the last 200 years has been one of massive expansion and growth. Little wonder, then, that Americans expect more from the market, and from business in general, than people in the rest of the world. In recent decades, with the freeing of international capital flows and increased globalisation, this optimistic outlook has taken hold of many other societies across the globe, while the opportunities in the US have somewhat decreased.

DEFINING IDEA...

We have a rule here that you can't go out and sell a product unless you can explain it in ten minutes.

– RUDOLPH DUTTWEILER, COMMERZBANK

In the UK the situation is a little different. We know in our hearts, even if we don't like to admit it to ourselves, that the UK has essentially a low growth economy controlled by a large public sector and an oligopoly of a few large companies. It is not at all easy for someone to build up a successful business from nothing in the UK. The spurts of growth that many UK investors tend to look for are in those few industries that suddenly become 'hot', and where a small firm can quickly make a fortune in a few years before the big boys muscle in – like mobile phones, for instance.

Either way – whether you are an optimist living in a high growth economy or a cynical opportunist living in a low growth economy – as an investor you are always on the lookout for a good story about a share. In other words, investors want to hear about companies that have, as Fred Schwed puts it, 'the promise of a little zip'.

The problem is that people who sell things – and believe me, people 'sell' securities just as hard as they sell anything else – know that there is a demand for a good story, and so they provide them. If you look at the financial columns or at share analysts' reports you will often find, in among the caveats, a description of a tantalisingly wonderful upside: if they find a second gold mine on the land they have bought … if the CXDS14 sells as well as the CXDS13 did … if Megabucks Corporation decides to buy them out … then investors will make a packet.

Most of the time, the big, tantalising, wonderful 'if's' don't work out, or if they do, they don't work out as well as expected, or something else happens to reduce the profits. Good stories are ten a penny. Finding a really well-run company that has a strong business that will go on making profits and getting bigger and bigger for many years is a much tougher proposition; they're rare, and no one can tell you which ones they are – you have to find out for yourself.

HERE'S AN IDEA FOR YOU...

The next time you read a good story about a company, check your reaction. Are you feeling, 'Oh my Gosh, I had better sell some of my other shares and fill my boots with this one'? Stop! You need to know much, much more about a company before you can make any kind of a judgement about whether or not it has a good chance of growing.

18 NANNY STATE?

'I have often heard it argued that this is a free country and if a rich man can take a flyer, why not a poor one? That is a good argument but I still don't agree with it and will therefore refuse to discuss it any further.'

DEFINING IDEA...

The easiest job I have ever tackled in the world is that of making Money. It is, in fact, almost as easy as losing it. Almost, but not quite.

– H.L. MENCKEN, HUMOURIST

The investment world offers the wealthy many fascinating and exciting ways of speculating with their money, from the foreign currency markets to fledgling biotechnology firms that might, just might, come up with a new wonder drug before they are launched on the stock market. Some of these opportunities are very highly geared, giving the investor the chance to borrow a huge multiple of the original stake, and thus greatly increasing the potential gain (or loss). When people read about these buccaneering activities, they often feel that it is unfair that only the rich seem to be allowed to play.

The truth is, though, that these activities are almost always very high risk. Rich people can, and often do, lose massive fortunes in such speculations. Hopefully they are rich enough to be able to bear the losses, but sometimes they aren't. When you lose, there is no one to hold your hand and sympathise. Maybe you have some grounds for complaint; perhaps some minor detail wasn't explained to you, or a clerk gave you slightly garbled information. Tough. Yes, you might be able to go to court, but it will cost a lot of money and you may lose, or worse still, you may win but not be able to collect.

Does anyone remember the Lloyds Names affair of the 1980s? For over a century wealthy landowners (who were asset-rich and cash-poor) used to guarantee the losses of insurance syndicates in return for a share of the insurance premiums; they were known as 'Names'. It was a nice little earner for a long time, but the danger was that a Name had to agree to unlimited liability. In other words, Names could potentially lose their entire wealth and still owe money. During the 1980s a series of massive insurance disasters, coupled with changes in the ethos and methods of Lloyds' insurance market, resulted in some of the insurance syndicates making extraordinarily large losses. A large number of Names lost everything without even making a dent in what they owed, and wound up living in caravans. They made a fuss, of course, and there were court cases, but there was a lot less sympathy and government help for them than would have been the case if they had been small savers who had lost their money. The feeling was, justifiably, that if you were so rich that you could afford to take such extraordinary risks, you should have been prepared to take the consequences when things went wrong.

HERE'S AN IDEA FOR YOU...

Whatever kind of financial venture you are contemplating, always ask yourself what your total potential exposure to loss would be, in the worst possible case. If it is more than the sum you are investing in the first place, you should probably think again.

19 JUST BECAUSE SOMEONE WORKS IN THE STOCK MARKET DOESN'T MEAN THEY ARE A GOOD INVESTOR

'Sometimes a number of rich men will band together and send one of their number in to pay for the service [of an investment adviser]. Then they will all use it. If it surprises you that there are millionaires who will stoop to such petty chiselling, then you should get out and meet more millionaires.'

DEFINING IDEA...

Wealth is the slave of a wise man, the master of a fool.

– SENECA

Money can make people ugly. Maybe they were ugly beforehand, or maybe the pursuit of money brought out the ugliness already in them, but the fact is that quite a lot of rich people are pretty unsavoury and unscrupulous in their business dealings. You only have to look at their private lives to see what a rotten lot many of them are. One multimillionaire of my acquaintance went to extraordinary lengths to disinherit his niece from a nice house in Manhattan that she had inherited from her father, the millionaire's brother. Here was a man who could have bought 50 such houses had he wanted to, and yet he spent years trying (successfully, as it turned out) to prise the only asset his niece had out of her hands.

There are other rich people who aren't like this at all. They're decent people with other interests apart from money. They care about their families, contribute to their communities and spend time on productive non-commercial activities, or at least they allow their nearest and dearest to do so – there are a lot of money-makers who are simply rather dull workaholics.

As is well known, with the boom in financial services across the world since the 1980s, a lot of financial professionals have grown rich, but what isn't so well known is that most of them haven't managed this by being brilliant market players. Most of them have been earning salaries and bonuses for doing more mundane jobs, like being good at getting customers to invest, or providing technical services, or being a good manager. All these are necessary jobs, but they don't have much to do with being a brilliant investor.

Then there are the traders – the young bloods who play the markets on behalf of their employers and get very well paid in the process. Surely they know a thing or two about investment? Not really – at least not about the kind of investment that outsiders can participate in. Most traders operate in an ultra short time-frame – often minutes, rather than days – and are focused on skimming profits on the movements of massive amounts of capital in markets such as foreign exchange; these are essentially wholesale markets that the ordinary investor can't participate in, at least not without a substantial disadvantage.

So, remember, just because someone is rich and is associated with the stock market, it doesn't mean he/she is a good investor.

HERE'S AN IDEA FOR YOU...

Don't think that just because someone is richer than you are that they know a lot about investment. Many, if not most, people acquire their wealth more by good fortune than through any extraordinary business acumen. And even people who are good at business can be bad – frequently very bad – at investment, so avoid 'hot tips' from rich people who seem to be in the know.

20 DIVERSIFICATION

'[The] claim is that by buying trust shares the modest investor is not forced to 'put all his eggs in one basket'. This argument sounds a good deal more reasonable than it actually is.'

Small investors are generally advised to diversify – i.e. to spread their money across a range of investments – and it is often said that by investing in a unit trust or an investment trust you can obtain better diversification than you could on your own. This is of course true, because these funds control millions of pounds which they can spread across a very large number of different companies and, indeed, asset classes.

DEFINING IDEA...
Wide diversification is only required when investors do not understand what they are doing.
– WARREN BUFFETT

To understand diversification, let's suppose there is an island with only two businesses, umbrellas and swimwear. When it rains, the umbrella company does well and when it is sunny, the swimwear company does well. The weather is unpredictable, so if you are completely invested in swimwear in a year when it rains all the time, your returns are going to be awful. By investing permanently in both the umbrella company and the swimwear company, you can be sure of making some kind of return whatever the weather – but it won't be as much as, say, investing in the swimwear company in a year with no rain.

What this doesn't tell us is how much diversification we actually need. More diversification is not necessarily better for us. Suppose you bought a share in every company on a stock exchange, including the secondary markets where small, often iffy, companies are quoted. You would then have a lot of diversification, you might think, but it would cost you a fortune in transaction fees. One celebrated theory, known as Modern Portfolio Theory, tells us that you don't really need to do this because a holding of as few as 20 shares will give you the diversification you really need.

The aim is really to diversify away the risk of something truly awful happening to your portfolio. When you diversify more than that, so the theory goes, all you are doing is reducing the returns you are likely to get without reducing the risk. So, for example, people who try to diversify by investing in lots of different unit trusts are wasting their time. As long as you have, say, £20,000 to invest, then you can obtain adequate diversification on your own. But if you don't want the bother of managing your investments yourself, then by all means invest in a few unit trusts or investment trusts – remember, though, that some of them are highly specialised and therefore do not provide good diversification.

HERE'S AN IDEA FOR YOU...

Some people worry a lot about diversification and then keep all their money in UK shares. That's not diversification. What about other parts of the world, Such as China and India, whose long term outlook appears to be very rosy? And what about the US, which still contains the majority of stock market value by capitalisation? To be properly diversified, you need to be exposed there too. So make sure you put some of your money into overseas markets, if only through a UK-based overseas investment trust.

21 HAVING YOUR CAKE AND EATING IT

'Perhaps what you are looking for is a long-range comprehensive investment program, conservative yet liberal, which will protect you from the effects of inflation and also deflation and which will allow you to sleep nights ... I will see to it personally that your inquiries are referred to the Head of our Crystal-Gazing Department.'

In most of his book, Fred Schwed is criticising the urge to speculate and the idea that you can spot a share that is going to go up, jump in and make a quick profit in a matter of a few weeks or months. Of course, this does happen sometimes, but it tends to be offset by the times when you jump in and make a quick loss. In this passage, however, Schwed is satirising a more bourgeois attitude: the desire for total security combined with a good return.

DEFINING IDEA...

Only buy something that you'd be perfectly happy to hold if the market shut down for ten years.

– WARREN BUFFETT

There is no such thing as zero risk. You do not know, for example, that there is no risk of you dropping dead tomorrow, or of the moon crashing into a giant asteroid. But these risks are so low, hopefully, that we can treat them as negligible. This is how financial risks are quantified. We take something that we think has almost 0% risk and use it as a benchmark against which to compare other things and determine their relative riskiness. For example, British government bonds, known as 'gilts' have been issued for more than 200 years and during that time the Bank of England has never been late in paying the coupon (the equivalent of interest) and has never defaulted on the principal amount. This means that gilts have a pretty good track record, especially if you compare them with, say, Russian government bonds, which have defaulted at least twice, or China's government bonds, which became worthless in the 1940s when Mao took over. So, we say that UK gilts have 0% risk, which isn't really true, because in the future some lunatic group might take over the government and repudiate its bonds – but we think and hope that this is unlikely to happen.

The next clever thing that financial wizards do is to say that risk is really volatility. In other words, risk is taken to mean how much a particular financial security, such as a share, tends to jump around in price. Small companies that focus on new technological inventions for example, tend to have quite high volatility – their shares jump up and down quite wildly. Some large firms, often called 'blue chips' just plod along without their share prices changing very much – or at least, that's what they're supposed to do – so to plan your portfolio, all you need to do is to decide on the right mix of volatility.

This isn't a bad plan, but what it can't give you is absolute certainty about what your performance is going to be like over the coming years. Nobody can do that.

HERE'S AN IDEA FOR YOU...

A lot of people want big gains in the stock market plus total security. You can't have both. We have to learn to live with uncertainty in investment, just as we do in the rest of life.

22 EXCEPTIONS ARE THE RULE

'… common stocks are speculative, preferred stocks are not nearly so speculative, debenture bonds are pretty darned safe, and mortgage bonds are safe. Unfortunately the exceptions to this are enormous and continual.'

DEFINING IDEA…

It's only when the tide goes out that you learn who's been swimming naked.

– WARREN BUFFETT

So, once we have decided on the relative riskiness of different kinds of stocks, we can lump them together accordingly. Thus, the conventional wisdom goes, certain government bonds, like those of the UK and the US, are taken to be absolutely safe, then other government bonds and various types of corporate bonds (for which there are ratings given by special agencies, such as Moody's and Standard and Poor's) which are a bit riskier, and then various classes of share, ranging from the not-very-risky to the extremely risky.

Now that we have done this we can decide on how much risk – actually volatility – we want to get involved with. The idea is that if we choose high volatility stocks we are more likely to get very good or very bad returns, while if we pick low volatility our returns will be more stable and predictable.

So why don't we bourgeois types just go for safe predictable government bonds? We know exactly what we can expect from them, because it is printed on the certificate that we get when we buy them – words to the effect of 'I promise to pay you X% a year for X years and give you your money back at the end.' That's a nice reliable promise. The trouble is that keeping all your money in government bonds will give you a lousy return, once you take inflation into account.

For this reason, most investors have to expose themselves to some degree of risk, usually by investing in shares. Often people want to invest in the 'blue chips', the giant corporations that are supposed to be less risky than other types of firm. But it isn't always the case that blue chip firms are safe.

Remember Enron? This was an energy company that grew rapidly in the 1980s and 1990s to become the seventh biggest company in the US. By 2000 it was called a 'blue chip', and its corporate bonds were AAA rated. Enron had become the darling of the stock market and was under extreme pressure to keep on producing wonderful results. To do this, it started to massage its accounts, first by using optimistic accounting methods and later by outright fraud. In late 2001 it was discovered that Enron had exaggerated its earnings by almost $600 million and that it secretly owed $3 billion to associated companies. Overnight, this blue chip company (seventh largest in the US, remember) saw its AAA bonds downgraded to junk, and over the next few months its share price fell from $85 to 30 cents. Enron's top notch accountancy firm, Arthur Andersen, was implicated in the wrongdoing and went out of business.

HERE'S AN IDEA FOR YOU...

During boom times corporate governance tends to get sloppy. Ordinary investors are told that everything is fine. Then, a few years later, it turns out that some firms were committing outrageous frauds. Try to develop your own instincts for smelling a rat, and remain cautious about the mega-success stories.

23 FUNDAMENTAL ANALYSIS

'The subject of choosing profitable investments does not lend itself to competence. There is almost no visible supply.'

Once again, Fred Schwed is ramming home his profound scepticism about the ability of financial professionals to choose good investments. As we have seen in the foregoing chapters, there is good reason for such scepticism, since, overall, professional fund managers don't seem to perform particularly well.

DEFINING IDEA...

Price is what you pay.
Value is what you get.
– WARREN BUFFETT

But let's take a closer look at how most professional fund managers approach the investment problem before dismissing them out of hand. The main method is called 'fundamental analysis', which is the idea that the careful study of the real businesses of listed companies can tell us something about which ones are likely to do well in the medium to long term. For example, if a company is steadily increasing its profits each year, we would expect this to be reflected in an increased share price. The aim of the fundamental analyst is to work out what a company 'ought' to be worth, by looking at its accounts, its business activities, its plans, its prospects and those of its competitors in the same industry.

The next step is to prepare detailed estimates of the company's likely future earnings and profits, taking into consideration possible changes in the costs of materials, labour and overheads and every other factor that might possibly have an effect. These estimates look very impressive, but you have to remember that they are only estimates, and are based on many assumptions that may or may not turn out to be accurate. So when you look at one of these reports, the main thing to establish is what these assumptions are; if the report doesn't tell you clearly, then it is not a good report.

The danger is, of course, that a detailed analysis of a company is only as good as the analyst who has made it. Someone with vast experience and intuitive knowledge of an industry may produce far better estimates than a wet-behind-the-ears analyst just out of business school, for instance, even though the former doesn't use the latest fancy jargon. A smart-looking report may seem to be very accurate, but it may be false precision – we can't really know for certain what the profits on product X in territory Y will be in, say, three years' time.

Even though fundamental analysis isn't an exact science, it does tell us a lot of useful things about companies. Don't try to apply it to every company you ever come across – it's too much work. Use it to deepen your grasp of the companies you are really interested in, which will generally be the ones you have invested in for the long term.

HERE'S AN IDEA FOR YOU...

Do you know your price/earnings (P/E) ratios? The P/E is measured as the price per share divided by the earnings per share. The higher the P/E, the more you are paying per unit of income – in other words, a high P/E share is more expensive. However, there may be good reasons for this. For example, companies whose earnings are growing strongly often have high P/Es. As a rule of thumb, when the stock market, or a particular sector, is trading at P/Es over 17, it's probably overvalued.

24 NEW ISSUES

'... the [SEC] felt that the public deserved to know every last detail of a new bond or stock issue ... In 1936–37 there was a boom on. The carefully scrutinized new issues went like hot cakes ... After that bull market ended, some of the scrutinized issues set modest records for the amount of money an investor could lose in a few weeks after subscribing to the issue.'

DEFINING IDEA...

Stocks have reached what looks to be a permanently high plateau.

– PROFESSOR IRVING FISHER, ECONOMIST, 1929, JUST BEFORE THE WALL STREET CRASH

Back in the bad old days of the Roaring Twenties, Fred Schwed tells us, the prospectuses for new issues, or Initial Public Offerings (IPOs) as they are now called in the US, did not give investors much information. It was almost as bad as the days of the South Sea Bubble in the early 1700s, when one enterprising promoter managed to raise thousands from the public 'for carrying on an undertaking of great advantage but no-one to know what it is'. Then, in the 1930s, the SEC began to insist on much more careful regulation of what could be said – and what had to be said – in a prospectus, and this still applies to most stock markets around the world today.

Schwed's point is that the net effect of all this well-intentioned effort on ordinary investors' returns hasn't been very noticeable. The prospectuses of new issues are now massive documents and incredibly dull, but they still can't tell you for certain whether a newly floated company is going to succeed. As the cost of making a new issue is enormous (because the company has to use specialist underwriters to conduct the issue and must spend a fortune on promotion and administration), companies tend only to launch new issues during a bull market. The aim is to make sure that the issue attracts enough subscribers (i.e. investors) to be a success, which is more likely when the market generally is going up. During bull markets one tends to see waves of new issues appearing, bunched together in hot industries, and often their share prices continue to rise for some time afterwards.

The acid test, though, is how such firms perform over the longer term. Often when the bull market ends the exciting new issue becomes a boring has-been, failing to perform impressively in its real business and losing its enthusiastic following. And that's what Fred is arguing: how different is it, really, from the bad old days when prospectuses didn't tell you anything?

New issues are as good as the companies that are behind them. Some are wonderful enterprises that go on to achieve bigger and better things. Others fail to live up to their promise. One thing is sure though – in most cases they are likely to be at the volatile end of the spectrum.

HERE'S AN IDEA FOR YOU...

This is one point you should always check when considering whether or not to invest in a new issue: what is the company going to do with the money it raises? Most of it should be going into developing the business. When the original shareholders are taking out more than 5% of the money raised for themselves, it is probably a bad sign.

25 TRUSTEES, EXECUTORS AND LAWYERS

'[There] is a tendency on the part of men in a fiduciary capacity (including trustees, executors and lawyers) to play so safe with client's funds that they just don't perform any useful service at all. They take the family's 100,000 dollars and invest it at a yield that is closer to zero percent than has ever been seen before.'

DEFINING IDEA...

Make crime pay.
Become a lawyer.
– WILL ROGERS, COMEDIAN

This is one of the great scandals of the investment business. Professional caretakers of money are much more worried about getting sued for misconduct or mismanagement than anything else, except possibly for ensuring that they pocket the fat fees they charge for their services. Any investment that is in the least bit volatile – in other words which may have a potential upside – is therefore to be avoided.

Not too much harm is done, perhaps, if these people are only looking after the money for a few months or a year, but if they are in charge for an extended period this ultra-conservative approach to money management can really make a dent in the capital sum. The fees, for some reason, are never regarded as damaging, although fees of a few thousand pounds can really eat into an estate of, say, £150,000 in the course of a few years.

Generations ago, when trusts weren't taxed as punitively as they are now, Edwardian gentlemen of means would create family trusts that were supposed to pass on money to their descendants, some of whom were not yet born. By the time inflation, new taxes, over-cautious investment and heavy trustees' fees had done their work, what had been intended as a nice lump sum to give a young person a good start in life turned out to be barely enough to buy an old banger.

The real problem, though, begins with the person who created the trust, or appointed the executors and lawyers, in the first place. Often it is an attempt to ensure some kind of equitable share of the wealth to descendants at some time after the person's death – usually because the descendants are still too young to be responsible about money. This is understandable, but hiring professionals to do the job is never ideal. A close friend, a trustworthy relative, someone with real integrity and sound judgement is a much better choice, if you want to make sure that your descendants really do get the money you want them to have. And don't try to play God; trusts can be overturned, so don't try to control the future too much after your death, or you may fail completely. You may wish for your children and grandchildren to grow up to be sensible about money, and to marry good spouses, but you can't force it to happen. Ultimately, it's their life, not yours, and you can't stop them from making mistakes.

HERE'S AN IDEA FOR YOU...

Today, creating a trust in the UK is probably inadvisable – they are just too expensive to run and too heavily taxed for most purposes. You might consider, though, creating a trust in another country that allows trusts. You can find them all over the world. Just remember, though, that trustees are always expensive creatures to feed, so make sure it is going to be worthwhile.

26 RETIREMENT PLANNING

'[To a bond trader] Tell me, Mac, what would you do if you had, today, two hundred and fifty thousand dollars of your own money?'

DEFINING IDEA...

The question isn't at what age I want to retire, but at what income.

– GEORGE FOREMAN, BOXER

The answer that the bond trader gives is an unwise one, but it highlights some key investment problems, so it is worth looking at in some detail. The trader first assumes that he will not live longer than another 25 years. Even in the 1940s that wasn't a particularly safe assumption and it is certainly unsafe to assume such a thing today. We really can't guess accurately how long we are going to live. The risk of being wrong by underestimating our life span is very serious. Winding up with no money in old age, when the cost of healthcare and nursing are only likely to increase and we are much more vulnerable to nasty shocks, is something you see all around you. Most of us would rather it didn't happen to us, so we should invest in such a way that our capital doesn't run out before we do!

Next, says the bond trader, he would take the $250,000 and divide it equally between twenty-five envelopes and put them in a safe. Every year he would remove one envelope, use half of it to gamble on the horses (gambling winnings are tax free) and live on the rest. Let's alter these figures to make them more meaningful in today's money: suppose you are given a lump sum of £2,500,000, and you put £100,000 in each of 25 envelopes, you spend £50,000 a year on the horses and live on the rest. Can you guess what is wrong with this picture?

The answer is: inflation. We have enjoyed low inflation for more than a decade, but there is no reason to believe that this happy state of affairs will continue for the next 25 years. A few bouts of high inflation, and by the twentieth year our bond trader might be having to live on envelopes that only had £12,500 in today's money, or even less.

The danger of inflation is the overriding reason why we have to invest lump sums and not just keep them under the bed. They won't keep their value otherwise. Over 25 years the interest on bank deposits certainly won't keep pace with inflation, most bonds will only barely do so. Assuming we would like our money to grow, we need to put it in the stock market and, if the UK housing market doesn't suffer any profound structural change, in houses too.

HERE'S AN IDEA FOR YOU...

Don't buy an annuity unless you have to. Although some pension schemes may require you to do so, these days annuities are usually optional. They are basically a kind of wager between you and an insurance company: you hand over a lump sum and the company promises to pay you a fixed amount (some schemes are inflation-adjusted) every year until you die. People who live much longer than expected make a profit, but it's probably better to keep control of your wealth and manage it on your own – the upside potential is better.

27 INDEX INVESTING

'Admittedly, it is preposterous to suggest that stock speculation is like coin flipping. I know that there is more skill in stock speculation. What I have never been able to determine is – how much more?'

DEFINING IDEA...

Most investors, both institutional and individual, will find that the best way to own common stocks is through an index fund that charges minimal fees.

~ WARREN BUFFETT, 1996

In chapter 13 the idea of index investing was mentioned. In the US this approach has become very widely used, with hundreds of billions of dollars going into special funds, known as tracker funds, which mimic one of the major indices, such as the NYSE or the S&P 500. It is quite telling that some 40% of institutional funds in the US, and slightly less in the UK, now goes into tracker funds.

Tracker funds are a passive, mechanical form of investment where the fund manager simply copies the target index by holding shares in all the companies in the index in the proportions in which they are weighted in that index. With the big indices this is sometimes impractical because of the number of companies included, in which case the fund holds what it hopes is a representative sample.

The whole idea of investing in this way is to gain returns that are very close to the performance of the index. Although stock markets do go through down patches, sometimes for years, over the long term the performance of the major indices has been good enough to generate a sound, inflation-beating return that has been superior to bonds or cash deposits, the two other main types of financial asset. Overall, this approach seems quite sound as an unexciting, conservative way of building up your assets over the long term.

The fees for a tracker fund ought to be considerably less than for an actively managed fund because the manager has much less to do, and there should be fewer transactions. With the funds that use representative samples, rather than buying shares in all the companies in the index, it is too early to tell just how representative these samples will really turn out to be. The less representative they are, the greater the 'tracking error', or difference, between the returns of the fund and the performance of the index.

Another point to remember is that these funds are probably not a great idea for short-term investing (actually, shares in general are not appropriate for short-term investing). For example, between 2000 and 2003 US shares lost an inflation-adjusted 6.8% a year, even though they gained 6.5% a year between 1900 and 2007.

HERE'S AN IDEA FOR YOU...

Although the idea of index investing makes a lot of sense, there are some potential problems. Some indices might be driven up to artificially high prices, followed by a crash, so you need to keep your eye on what is happening in the index fund market. And if the Western economies are going to go downhill in the course of a 'hegemonic shift' towards Asia, as some people like to predict, then the big US and UK indices may not perform very well in the future. Lastly, there are already some daft index funds that try to do a bit of active management at the same time – that's not the point, so avoid them.

28 DON'T INVEST ON A HIGH

'The habit of buying popular shares works for bad results ... It must tend to get the buyer in nearer the top than the middle.'

What could be stupider than buying high and selling low? But that is what most investors do. They wait until all the news about the stock market is wonderful and prices are high, and then pile in. Much later, when the stock market has been sliding for a long time, all the news is doom and gloom and prices are low, investors lose their nerve and get out of the market.

DEFINING IDEA...

Your goal as an investor should simply be to purchase, at a rational price, a part interest in an easily-understandable business whose earnings are virtually certain to be materially higher five, ten and twenty years from now.

– WARREN BUFFETT

It would be great to be able to time the market perfectly, to buy just as the stock market, or a particular share, had reached its lowest point and was just about to embark on a long climb upwards, and to sell just as prices had reached their absolute peak and were about to fall, but it really can't be done. But much of the benefit can be gained

from being approximately right – in other words, from buying lowish and selling highish, which is a bit easier to do, for some people at least.

For example, at the time of writing, the FTSE 100 is at just under 5,000. Back at its peak in 2007 it was over 6,500. If I invested in the index now and it ever got back to its 2007 peak, I would make a return of around 30%. Currently the economic news is a little more optimistic than it has been for a while. Are we anywhere near a low? Who knows? Are we lower than we were two years ago? Absolutely. Do I think that at some point in the future share prices will go even higher than they were in 2007? Yes! If I am right, this tells me that if I invest now, at some point in the future there is at least a 30% return to be had – but of course, how good a gain that turns out to be depends on the length of time it takes to get there, and what happens to inflation during the period.

Deciding when a stock market is too high is probably more difficult. A good rule of thumb is that when all the dimmest, most arrogant people you know are bragging about how great the stock market is, it's probably a good time to start getting out!

HERE'S AN IDEA FOR YOU...

A good business is still a good business – and there really aren't that many of them – even in an overheating stock market, but if its share price has been inflated by general optimism, it'll be an expensive business to invest in. And that means it will take longer before you see some really substantial gains. When the market is declining, however, you can sometimes pick up fabulous companies for much less than they are 'really' worth. So keep an eye out for those companies who you think are really well-run firms with a good future for growth.

29 COMPANIES DON'T OFTEN TURN AROUND

'The true speculator starts near the corner of Wall and Broad and doesn't wander farther away than the next two ticker [machines]. He knows that in some savage unvisited spot like New Jersey a corporation is actually in business, but he doesn't really think that important.'

Sometimes you see articles about some well-regarded managers who are bringing in a new team to sort out some tired industrial behemoth and put it back on its feet. This is often called a 'turnaround' situation. The fact is, most turnarounds (more than 70%) don't succeed.

DEFINING IDEA...

Both our operating and our investment experience cause us to conclude that 'turnarounds' seldom turn.

~ WARREN BUFFETT

Why should this be? One reason is that large companies have large bureaucracies, and these behave much more like inefficient government departments (my vote for least efficient goes to the DSS) than you might imagine. Poorly performing companies are often rotten from the inside, with dismal buildings, second-rate employees, bad habits, a flaccid corporate culture and little positive leadership. They find it difficult to respond to a changing market place; one company I know of hasn't changed the way in which it defines its customers in nearly 50 years, which is just asking for trouble.

If you don't believe in hopeless cases, think of British Rail, or the Royal Mail. They developed a lot of bad habits back in the days when they were fully in the public sector, and although successions of dynamic executives have tried to change things from the top, the situation hasn't improved much.

The Royal Mail suffers from another serious problem too: its whole business is seriously under threat. The only letters most of us ever receive these days are junk mail and bills. Most of our correspondence is through email, and most of our salaries and invoices go directly into our accounts by bank transfer. When we send a parcel, it is often by a private carrier. When, as a company, your whole *raison d'être* is being undermined, it may take a miracle to change things. And the Royal Mail seems to be in no position to be getting one any time soon.

It is not just former public sector outfits that get into this kind of trouble. There are lots of dinosaur industries. Think of the car manufacturers. There are too many of them, making too many cars, and there is mounting pressure to do something about their negative contribution to climate change. It's a potent political issue, and of course there are lots of vested interests who don't want anything to change. Not all the car manufacturers can survive, and the ones that do will probably do so by developing newer, cleaner technology for the mass market. But unless you are truly expert on the car industry, it's difficult to see which, if any of the world's large manufacturers are a good investment for the long term.

HERE'S AN IDEA FOR YOU...

When you are a senior executive in charge of fixing an ailing business, you must try and do it. But as a private investor you are not in that unenviable position. You don't have to figure out how to do the impossible. You can just walk away and invest in some other business that is actually going places.

30 RIDE THE WINNERS

'My tendency has been to buy stocks, all a-tremble as I do so. Then when they show a profit, I sell them, exultantly. (But never within six months, of course. I'm no anarchist.)'

DEFINING IDEA...
Orgies tend to be wildest toward the end.
– WARREN BUFFETT

Let's suppose that you just can't help it, and you have to try your hand at picking shares for yourself. Well, at least you'll be saving a lot of expensive fund management fees. Here's one method of going it alone that some people swear by – for reasons that will become obvious, it works best in a bull market.

First, pick a number of shares in substantial companies that you believe are well run and have good prospects and, crucially, that have a track record of good performance for at least three years. Tell yourself that you are going to keep them for a minimum of three and more probably eight or more years, UNLESS they start to perform badly.

Next, check your share prices regularly. Every day is preferable, but every week will do. If nothing happens for a long time, that's fine. If one of your companies gets taken over, take the cash and don't keep any shares in the new, merged company. Use this cash to invest in another good performer. When one of your shares starts to perform poorly, try to find out why: read the specialist financial press and try to establish just what the problem seems to be. If it looks like a long term problem, or the share price drops significantly, sell it and forget it.

The next rule is, don't touch the winners! Let them keep on going up. Maybe they go into the doldrums for a year or two. Don't worry – as long as they don't actually start dropping in price substantially and there is no good reason to believe that there is something fundamentally wrong, just wait. The temptation to take your profits may be immense, especially if you have, say, doubled your money on a particular share. Don't succumb to this feeling; sometimes your winners will just keep on growing and growing, and for your overall portfolio to do well you need some winners like these.

Many people find riding their winners one of the hardest things to do in investment. They don't have the courage of their convictions. But if you really believe that Company X is a fabulous company, wouldn't you want to hold it forever, or at least until it changes fundamentally for the worse?

HERE'S AN IDEA FOR YOU...

Riding the winners and dumping the losers is essentially a short-termist trading strategy. Although it may work for portfolios that are less than expertly picked, if you really believe in your shares – because you have studied them properly, with your business brain in gear – then there shouldn't be much that happens that should change your mind, and you ought to be willing to hold onto great companies through some lean times. However, as a psychological trick to keep you from buying and selling too often, it's probably okay as a creed.

31 THE TROUBLE WITH TRANSACTION COSTS

'The man who chooses to take his money and churn it furiously … cannot in any way predict his fate, save for a single assurance. So long as any money still clings to the side of the churn, he will not be bored.'

People who have never owned shares often imagine that investors spend their time buying and selling every day, if not every hour – and they also imagine that this is fun. That might be okay if you are a large institution with a department full of traders with nothing else to do, because financial institutions pay very low transaction charges. For the private investor, though, it's an expensive activity, because the transaction costs are higher, so the more you trade, the more the charges eat into your overall return.

What's worse, if you like to speculate in less well-known companies, like the ones quoted on AIM (the Alternative Investment Market) or the OTC (the Over The Counter market), you'll find that the 'spread' can be very much wider than in the main market – that's the difference between the price at which a dealer will buy from you (the 'bid') and the price at which he will sell to you (the 'offer'). For this reason ordinary investors should try to keep the number of transactions they make to a minimum. If you have invested well, there is often no reason to buy and sell even once a year.

Regulators have strict rules designed to prevent brokers and other financial professionals from 'churning' their clients' accounts. 'Churning' simply means buying and selling securities too frequently, in order to generate commissions. Although the rules are strict, there are lots of ways of encouraging people to churn. For example, your bank restructures its departments and you have a new investment manager, who asks to see you, hums and haws at your portfolio, and then suggests you sell everything and buy a bunch of other things. Or you inherit a portfolio and the same thing happens.

Eager investors, however, don't need much encouragement to churn their portfolios – they do it all too willingly, all by themselves. Don't be one of them. The stock market is not like a computer game that gives instant gratification; it's more like gardening, and takes a lot of patience.

HERE'S AN IDEA FOR YOU...

The old-fashioned stockbrokers are becoming a thing of the past, which is a shame because although they were quite expensive, they were often very good and could teach you a lot about the markets. Then came the 'execution-only' brokers, who were cheaper but didn't give you any advice. And now there are the online brokers, who offer really cut-rate, low cost dealing charges. Online broking has matured in recent years and now the services they offer are generally pretty good, and you can often trade for a flat rate of as little as £12. Remember though, you'll be getting no advice, so make sure you have got your facts absolutely right before you make the trade, or you could end up buying the wrong thing, or the wrong amount, by mistake.

32 CROOKS

'The crookedness of Wall Street is in my opinion an overrated phenomenon.'

It all depends on how you define crookedness. On the broadest level – of intellectual dishonesty, say – one might argue that almost the entire financial services industry, with very few exceptions, is dishonest because it is based on a number of false or misleading premises. Here are some examples:

The fund management business, by and large, not only promotes the idea that active fund managers have a superior ability in stock-picking (which, as we have seen, is not borne out by the evidence) but also connives at producing misleading information about past performance by constantly merging and closing funds, and opening new ones. Stock brokers (often now departments of larger institutions) encourage customers to 'churn' their portfolios, which means to buy and sell securities for no good reason, thus generating extra commissions for the broker. Insurance companies operate various kinds of complex savings-cum-insurance schemes that are poor value for many customers, and, in territories where regulation is lax, make very misleading claims about these schemes. Organisations that have the most to do with the public, like banks and building societies, produce misleading literature about the benefits of their savings accounts and actively promote disinformation to the less sophisticated sections of society. All this is true in every one of the 17 countries in which I have worked in the financial services industry, although the degree and nature of the abuses vary from country to country.

Ok, maybe, just maybe, this kind of thing is no worse than what goes on in any industry. The goings on in the double-glazing business, or in poorly run pubs, may be just as bad. So let's be generous and just call all of the above 'questionable practices'. What about the real crooks? They may be in a minority, as Schwed rightly says. Often they seem to start out with good intentions but slowly get drawn into fiddling that mushrooms over the years into a gigantic fraud.

Here are just a few of the prominent characters from the Rogues' Gallery during the last few years: Bernie Madoff, arrested in December 2008 for running a fraudulent investment scheme that collapsed owing more than 60 billion dollars; Bernard Ebbers, former CEO of Worldcom, a large telecommunications company, jailed in 2005 for false financial reporting that resulted in a loss of some 11 billion dollars to investors; Jack Grubman, a stock analyst who was fined and banned for life from the securities industry in 2004 for producing over-optimistic reports and ratings on some of the companies he followed; David Walsh, founder of Bre-X Mining, which went bankrupt in 1997 after it was discovered that a gold mine it owned in Borneo had been fraudulently 'salted' with gold; Michael Milken, father of the junk bond industry, convicted of insider trading in 1989. The list just goes on and on, but you get the idea: yes there are crooks around in the stock market – lots of them!

HERE'S AN IDEA FOR YOU...

Your best defence from being cheated is information. Read and learn about how financial frauds happen, and inoculate yourself against the disease of gullibility.

33 AVOIDING THE BIG COLLAPSES

'… an effort to put a little truth into the falsest text in the English language: "God tempereth the wind to the shorn lamb". He doesn't, you know. Look about you.'

Continuing with the theme of the previous chapter, what do you do if you are unfortunately caught up in a major fraud or an honest collapse? Sadly, victims are pretty much like 'shorn lambs' and the wind blows pretty hard on them. Has anyone got their money back from the Icelandic banks yet? I suppose they will, eventually.

DEFINING IDEA…

The basic dishonest scheme was simple and as old as the hills. You persuade people to entrust their savings to you by telling them that they will be kept safe … You don't put the money in a rock-solid investment but use it to live the life of Riley.

– PROSECUTOR IN THE BARLOW CLOWES CASE

Although the better regulated countries, of which Britain is one (although you might not think so), provide various compensation schemes to protect investors, there are always exceptions (things that aren't covered by the scheme) and it often takes years before you get all or part of your money back. From January 2010, the FSA (the UK's regulator) has covered investments of up to £50,000 with the scheme. But having to wait and worry is no fun, which is why there was a run on the Northern Rock bank in 2007; people didn't have much confidence in the compensation scheme, and rightly so!

What can we do to avoid these kinds of problems? There is no cast iron method for avoiding loss, but here are a few things you can do to minimise the risks:

First, don't put all your savings into one scheme. For example, if only the first 50,000 of any investment is covered by a compensation scheme, then don't put more than 50,000 in. It may be tiresome to have several accounts, but it is a necessary precaution.

Second, follow the news about the institutions that you invest with. Read the financial press, the trade press and the blogs. We may not have complete freedom of speech, but we aren't completely muzzled either. You usually hear from a few doubting Thomases long before a firm goes bust. For example, in the case of the Madoff fraud, the firm was paying its investors relatively high returns (around 10%) for what was supposed to be relatively low risk. As some people were pointing out years before the collapse, there was something a bit fishy about this – Madoff was supposed to be doing fancy things with derivatives, yet the returns weren't at all volatile, which they should have been.

Third, look closely at what is being offered. Does it make sense? For example, in the Barlow Clowes affair of the 1980s, the good returns were said to be created by 'bond washing', a legitimate technique to reduce taxes, but when it was outlawed the firm claimed to have other techniques to keep the returns high. Just what these other techniques were was never properly explained.

HERE'S AN IDEA FOR YOU...
If you do get caught in a collapse, get involved with the activist groups and make sure that you are named in any class action suits. But don't devote your life to it – get on with living.

34 COUNTER-CYCLICAL INVESTMENT

'When there is a stock market boom ... take all your common stocks and sell them. Take the proceeds and buy conservative bonds ... just wait for the depression which will come sooner or later. When [the] depression comes ... sell out the bonds (perhaps at a loss) and buy back the common stocks ... Continue to repeat this operation as long as you live.'

As discussed in chapter 30, it would be great if we could discipline ourselves to buy low and sell high. That is what a particular group of specialists try to do – they are known as 'counter-cyclical' investors. When gold, property or bonds are low, for instance, they buy, and when shares are low they sell their holdings and load up on shares.

DEFINING IDEA...

Never follow the crowd.

– BERNARD BARUCH.
FAMOUS INVESTOR

For people who like this kind of approach, it is important to look further afield than the conventional investment areas – for example to the volatile markets of the Far East. In recent decades, with the advent of globalisation, many of these markets have lurched up and down alarmingly as massive amounts of foreign capital has poured in, taken fright, and poured out again. Take Indonesia, for example. Since 1998 it has had quite a wild ride: at its bottom in September 1998 the main index, the JKSE, was at around 263, rising to 707 in June 1999; from a low of 360 in 2002, it soared, almost without a glitch, to 2,657 in December 2007, before dropping to 1,348 in December of the following year and then recovering to 2,300 in August 2009.

Counter-cyclical investors love this kind of volatility. Indonesia is a populous country with an extraordinary wealth of natural resources, and you might feel that the country is a reasonable bet, that in spite of its problems its main firms are going to be kept going by whatever regime happens to be in power. Risky? Certainly, but look at the potential rewards: if you had invested at roughly the right times, you could have multiplied your money many times over. And to make sure that you actually got your money out without problems you could have invested in one of the specialist funds, based elsewhere, that focus on the country.

Counter-cyclical investment takes guts. Your friends and neighbours are going to think you are crazy. Do yourself a favour and don't tell them what you are doing. You don't need their advice. But do write down your rationale before you invest, and refer to it from time to time. When you have no one to talk to, you need to keep records of what you were thinking if you want to stay disciplined. When you start second-guessing yourself all the time, you can easily start trading too often, and wind up making a loss.

HERE'S AN IDEA FOR YOU...

Another possibility is to look for undervalued assets outside the stock market. For example, Jim Rogers, the erstwhile partner of George Soros, the billionaire trader who forced sterling out of the European Exchange Mechanism in 1990, is bullish on commodities. According to Rogers, these basic items, such as sugar, coffee, oil and copper, have nowhere to go but up in the long term. Maybe he is right – but play it safe, and don't gamble on margin. Keep your investments within safe limits and look for modest, steady gains.

35 GLOBALISATION

'Now, whatever the reader may think of totalitarian philosophy in general, I don't think he will envy them for the condition of their security markets.'

DEFINING IDEA...

We have the most magnificent lithium reserves on the planet, but if we don't step into the race now, we will lose this chance. The market will find other solutions for the world's battery needs.

~ BOLIVIAN ECONOMIST

There has been a lot of talk about the evils of globalisation in recent years, and it has been blamed for everything from child labour to an attempt to create single world government. It is certainly not a pretty sight to see ancient ways of life disappearing, to fly across the whole of Asia at night and see nothing but street lights all the way, or to watch the burgeoning youth of the Third World learn to gorge itself on junk food. But most of this didn't start with globalisation, it started with the Industrial Revolution, more than 150 years ago, when Western-made consumer goods first started being rammed down the throats of consumers in other countries. And now, at least, some of these countries have got in on the act and are ramming their mass-produced goods down our throats – and people are complaining about that too!

Globalisation gets blamed for the problems of modernity, which is unfair. Modernity is a phenomenon that began a long time before we were born and will go on for a long time after we are dead. Globalisation, by comparison, is a flash in the pan; it began in a small way in the 1980s and may be already past its prime. Some of us can remember what things were like before it started. Back in the post-war period – say, 1945 to the 1980s – international business was extremely restricted. If you went to a foreign country, getting money from home was a huge problem. At one point it was illegal to take more than £50 out of the UK, which was barely enough for a weekend in Calais.

Restrictions, rules and customs duties were everywhere. If you wanted to invest in a promising business in another country, there was a very real danger that you wouldn't be allowed to take your profits home. Consequently, investors refused to invest in many countries where consumers were screaming out for basic goods, and business people were eager to supply them, but couldn't, for lack of capital.

Globalisation changed all that. By lifting the restrictions on investment flows between countries, reducing barriers to trade, encouraging the development of stock markets and making it easier for firms to set up manufacturing operations in countries with cheaper labour, huge incentives to be more productive were created, and there has been a real growth in the world's prosperity.

As a whole, much of the world, including much of the developing world, lives longer, eats better, gets better medicine and better education than it did in the past – and we investment folk think that globalisation has helped this process.

HERE'S AN IDEA FOR YOU...

If you want to understand how businesses work make a study of the effects that governments can have on how markets function. And visit countries where things work differently from the way they do in the UK. It'll give you a much better understanding of where the opportunities are.

36 NUMERACY REQUIRED

'Wall Street has always been burdened by having among its personnel a good many otherwise estimable people who don't know anything about the laws of probabilty and risk, and not too much about arithmetic.'

Chapter 9 introduced the idea that it might be a good idea to know a little about probability and statistics if you want to invest in the stock market. In this chapter let's look at one of the important concepts in measuring your investment performance: the concept of risk adjustment.

DEFINING IDEA...

Take calculated risks. That is quite different from being rash.
– GEORGE PATTON. WW2 GENERAL

As we know, any investment in equities involves risk. In investment this risk is often defined as the risk that your actual returns are different from the expected return. So, what returns should you expect from a given stock or portfolio of stocks? To understand how one might estimate the expected return, first consider what you can expect from a 'risk-free' investment such as US government bonds.

Suppose you can invest in US bonds for one year and receive a guaranteed return of 5%: your expected return is 5%, and at the end of the year you find that you have indeed received an actual return of 5%.

Now, let's consider what happens in an equity investment. You calculate an expected return from a given investment (this is done by calculating the standard deviation of past returns) and buy the stock. When the time comes to sell, it is quite probable that your actual returns will not be exactly the same as your expected return; if they are a little lower, or a lot higher, most investors will be happy with the results, but if they are considerably lower than the expected return, most investors will feel that they have made an error.

We can say that a company with wild price swings is riskier than a stable one because it is harder to predict its expected return; another way of saying this is that its actual returns have had a higher 'variance' from the expected return. If we only calculate the average of past annual return figures for a firm, we may not appreciate just how risky a company with high variance really is – 'risk' means how likely a given annual return is to be much higher or lower than the average. A company with high variance might have an average return over the past 10 years of, say 5%, which sounds boring and respectable.

But if we don't look at the variance, we might be in for some very big surprises. For example, we might find that one year we got an amazing 27% return and in other years we actually lost money.

Of course we all hope to make a killing by plunging in and out of shares at the right time, but in the major markets, the odds are very much against us – so get used to measuring them!

HERE'S AN IDEA FOR YOU...

When you look at price charts you often see quite fantastic leaps and drops, often for reasons you can't fathom. You may not know where the price is going to go next year, but you can work out the variance of its performance in the past, which gives you an estimate of how wildly this stock might leap. You might want to stick to steady stocks with the same long term performance.

37 SHORT SELLING

'Before October 1929 no-one objected to short sellers except their own families. They objected to going bankrupt.'

Fred Schwed devotes a good deal of his book to defending short sellers, who got a lot of blame for the Wall Street Crash of 1929. It is hilarious to find the same kinds of attacks on short sellers happening today, 90 years and umpteen crashes later.

DEFINING IDEA...

But now that prices are coming down, I don't hear anybody saying hedge funds have done a good job bringing down the price of oil.

– PHIL GOLDSTEIN, BULLDOG INVESTORS (A HEDGE FUND)

But first, we should understand what short sellers do. They borrow shares – or other securities – from their owners and then sell them in the market. The idea is that if the price falls, they can buy the securities back at the lower price, give them back to the owner and keep the difference as a profit. You can achieve the same result by betting that a security will go down using derivatives contracts. To be able to short, there has to be a counter-party – someone who is willing to bet that you are wrong – and you are taking a major risk. In Fred Schwed's opinion, any money that a short seller makes is well-deserved, given the risks and the fact that a lot of the time they lose a fortune.

Nobody minds about short sellers most of the time, but when there is a bear market (i.e. one that is going down) it is obviously a better opportunity for them to try to make some money. Then everyone complains about 'bear raiding', and says that it is damaging the economy. These days the big short sellers are the hedge funds, who got a lot of flack when HBOS shares fell over 20% in March 2008; it was claimed that short sellers were deliberately trying to manipulate the market by spreading false rumours about the bank. An investigation by the Financial Services Authority was unable to find any concrete evidence of wrongdoing, which isn't that surprising – the market is ALWAYS full of false rumours, at all times. During the same period, a short seller named David Einhorn was giving lectures in the US about what he thought was wrong with Lehman Brothers' accounts. In September 2008 Lehman collapsed, owing hundreds of billions. The SEC sprang into action and investigated Einhorn for evidence that he was trying to manipulate the stock. They found none. Of course not! Bear raiders don't have to manipulate the shares of a company that is on the way out – they just have to make the bet.

Short sellers provide liquidity to the market and take enormous risks when doing so. They really are not a bad thing. Even Warren Buffett, who doesn't short much himself, thinks they are useful because they seek out problems in companies, especially in their accounts, that other people are trying to keep under wraps.

HERE'S AN IDEA FOR YOU...

Short selling really, really isn't for amateurs, because timing is everything; if you are just a little bit wrong you can lose a packet. Don't try it – but if you must, why not try shorting through a spread betting company? Then at least any profits that you make will be tax free.

38 THOSE CRAZY REGULATORS

'I find myself wishing that the [Securities and] Exchange Commission would perform its functions with a little less zip and hurrah.'

DEFINING IDEA...

The crisis of yesterday is the joke of tomorrow.

~ H.G. WELLS

The SEC, and its counterpart in the UK, are vulnerable to political interference, especially in times of economic crisis. They have to look as if they are pursuing wrongdoers ruthlessly, even when it isn't very clear who the wrongdoers are, or even if there are any. It is not an easy job, because people are always complaining that the regulators are either too lax or too zealous. The SEC is usually accused of being overzealous, and of hounding perfectly innocent people, while the FSA (and its predecessors) have often been seen as toothless and afraid to act.

But then again, the SEC has been roundly criticised for investigating Bernie Madoff (see chapter 32) several times without finding much wrong (after a number of complaints) before the firm finally collapsed, revealing the biggest fraud in history. And lately the FSA has been getting very tough with some of the smaller players, for example by fining Thinc Group, a financial adviser, £900,000 in 2008 for misselling subprime mortgages.

Maybe they do these things better in China. Over there, financial miscreants are sometimes executed. But the reality is that regulators have a nearly impossible job. Yes, you can regulate people into the ground, but then the financial world would spend all its time filling in forms instead of doing any business – and that would be bad for the economy, bad for borrowers and bad for investors.

What tends to happen is that regulatory controls get a bit laxer during booms, and a bit tighter during crashes. In a crash everybody wants to make sure that it will never happen again. In 2002 the Sarbanes-Oxley Act was introduced to prevent the kinds of accounting abuses that had been rife in the preceding boom. We were all supposed to breathe a sigh of relief and believe that bad practices were a thing of the past. What happened? Even worse abuses started to appear in another area (banking) during the next boom.

So what will happen next? The really big problem seems to be in the growth of derivatives, because according to some respectable estimates, the world's derivatives exposure is now more than 20 times the world's GDP. That's an unimaginably large figure (more than 1 quadrillion dollars), and it is happening in a non-transparent, unregulated market that no regulator has the power to control. What needs to happen is for governments and regulators across the world to get together and create a system that forces derivatives players to account for these deals clearly and in a manner that the regulators can supervise.

HERE'S AN IDEA FOR YOU...

The danger to the world's financial system posed by derivatives is a good reminder that we should spread our money across different asset classes. It's a good idea hold a few valuable things, like gold sovereigns, that can be used to buy things in times of really serious financial chaos. Remember, towards the end of World War II in Europe, there was so little money around that people used cigarettes instead of cash. These things can happen!

39 COLLECTIVE INVESTMENTS

'If investment [and unit] trusts would only function in actuality anything like as well as they do in theory, they would be a tremendous asset to the general welfare.'

Neither Fred Schwed nor I think that collective investments are likely to achieve consistently outstanding performance. But nevertheless there are a lot of them, and it is worth knowing something about them because they can sometimes be useful for a specific purpose.

DEFINING IDEA...

His promises were, as he then was, mighty; But his performance, as he is now, nothing.

– WILLIAM SHAKESPEARE, HENRY VIII

So what are collective investments, exactly? They are pooled investments that take money from many investors and put them into a single investment portfolio, managed by professional fund managers. The first such funds appeared in the 1820s, so they have been going for a long time, and they are very strictly regulated (hedge funds, arguably, are different in this respect – see chapter 46). Many funds are forbidden by law from making risky investments. There are two main types – 'Closed-end' funds, known in the UK as investment trusts, which have shares quoted on the stock exchange, and 'Open-end' funds, known as mutual funds in the US and as unit trusts in the UK. Open-end funds sell units in the fund, which are not traded on a stock exchange, directly to the investor. The difference is important because you can often buy shares in a closed-end fund at a discount to the total value of their assets, which most people would think was a bargain.

There are now tens of thousands of funds on the world market. They are not all the same! Their objectives and the risks they take to achieve them, vary very widely indeed. You can buy a fund that invests in a specific country or industry, one that only buys bonds, one that tries to have a balance between shares and bonds, and so on, ad infinitum. There are even 'funds of funds', which only buy other funds – which doesn't make any sense to me, since the fees are inevitably considerably higher. A typical equity fund charges between 1.5% and 2.5% a year, which is already on the steep side.

As mentioned in chapter 27, most funds choose a benchmark, such as a stock market index, against which their fund's performance can be judged. For the comparison to be meaningful, you need to assess whether the fund's investments are genuinely similar to the benchmark. For example, a fund may be managed in a way that is not closely aligned to its benchmark in order to achieve better performance. For this reason, it is useful to compare a fund's performance with those of similar funds as well as with its chosen benchmark.

HERE'S AN IDEA FOR YOU...

Read the prospectus before investing – it's absolutely vital that you know what you are getting into! The prospectus will tell you how long it will take for you to receive your money when you sell, how much the charges are, all the special conditions, its past performance and a breakdown of its holdings by size. You need to know all these things before piling in. Suppose you want to make a bet on Taiwan going up by investing through a fund – you need to make sure that a fund called 'The Taiwan Fund' actually does invest in representative companies.

40 MERGERS AND ACQUISITIONS

'Just what authority do you have … to criticise the mental qualities of a man who has made thirty million dollars?' I figure I have the same authority as the fan at a ball game who yells 'You big dope!' when the Yankee short-stop scoops up a [ball] and throws it to the wrong base.'

Mergers and acquisitions (M&A) mainly occur during booms, so there isn't much going on in this area at the moment, but it is a good time to start researching the subject. When things start to improve, there will be a marked increase in M&A activity, giving some good short-term investment opportunities.

DEFINING IDEA...

Mega-mergers are for megalomaniacs.

– DAVID OGILVY, FOUNDER OF OGILVY & MATHER ADVERTISING

An M&A happens when two firms combine, either by friendly agreement or because one firm manages to get enough of the existing shareholders in the target company to sell it their shares. Sometimes a firm just buys the assets of another firm, and sometimes the existing managers borrow a vast sum to take over the firm themselves.

When you are a shareholder in a company that is 'in play', and other firms are competing to pay the biggest price for your shares, you are lucky; most of the time it's best to sell your shares and get out with a nice profit.

The rationale for M&A is supposed to be that the new, combined business will be better and stronger. That may be true when a giant in an industry is gobbling up all the smaller players and the industry is being rationalised, but otherwise they often don't work out very well. For the investor, the main point is that an acquisition needs to have a good, value-adding business reason if you are going to hang on to your shares in the combined firm.

So if mergers often don't work, why do people make them happen? The answer seems to be that for the senior executives involved it's all very exciting and glamorous – and often they stand to gain a fortune personally. Executives in the outgoing board may be given fantastically generous 'golden parachutes' that mean they never have to work again. For example, Ross Johnson, the CEO of Nabisco, engineered a merger with RJ Reynolds in 1986, and after the combined company performed poorly, engineered another one with a leveraged buyout firm in 1988 and got out with a 53.8 million dollar payoff.

M&A activity is associated with bull markets; if the real motive were to pick up a bargain, one would expect to see more takeovers in bear markets, since the purchase cost would be much, much lower. And if you don't believe all this, would you like to hazard a guess at which industry had the most merger activity during the boom that led up to the 2007 banking crisis? That's right – it was the American banking industry!

HERE'S AN IDEA FOR YOU...

Buy the target firms, sell on the merger. Don't believe any stories about how wonderful the new firm is going to be unless it really, really makes sense. How to find a potential target? Look in industries where a lot of mergers have been happening recently, especially those where there are ongoing technological and market changes, and pick the juiciest-looking firms.

41 MASSAGING THE FIGURES

'I doubt if there are many, or any, Wall Streeters who sit down and say to themselves coolly, 'Now let's see. What cock and bull story shall I invent and tell them today?'

DEFINING IDEA...

Earnings can be pliable as putty when a charlatan heads the company reporting them.
– WARREN BUFFETT

When the stock market is doing well, many top executives become obsessed with what the market thinks about their firm's performance. When analysts are screaming for an improved profit figure every quarter, a lot of executives start to feel that they have to provide them, by whatever means. In some ways, therefore, it is better for business when the stock market is off the boil, because the pressure is off and managers can get on with important things, like making the business better and stronger, instead of trying to cook the books. The committed shareholders will hang on to their shares anyway, because they believe in the business.

Doing things to the accounts to make them match analysts' expectations is known as 'earnings management'. It involves misleading, but not necessarily illegal, accounting manoeuvres. Cisco Systems, for example, once reported earnings exactly one penny per share above analysts' predictions for 13 consecutive quarters! The chance of this happening without some form of earnings management is tiny. Analysts and regulators can usually only spot the most obvious kinds of earnings management, and often they don't seem to mind it (as in the case of Cisco).

What's worse, stock markets often punish companies that do not meet analysts' expected earnings figures. It is not that the analysts make good predictions, it's just that a lot of investors read them, and if the actual figures are worse then expected, they sell their shares, often causing the price to drop substantially.

So, how is it done? There are lots of ways. They involve adjusting the entire range of the company's financial statements, by changing earnings recognition policies, depreciation methods and depreciation timetables, deciding how much to allow for uncollectible receivables, estimating write-downs for investments, deciding on future liabilities as a result of litigation or environmental regulation. These kinds of figures can be changed quite easily, and relatively legitimately, so that you end up with the results you want the market to see.

Why do they have to do it? The reasons vary, and are often to do with the everyday problems that all businesses have to deal with. Suppose a big customer delays a final payment on a contract; the quarterly revenue figures will be down, which will look bad to the market. Or perhaps the debt to equity ratio of the firm has increased to a level that triggers higher interest payments on the company's bonds – the incentive to massage down the debt-to-equity ratio will be quite strong.

HERE'S AN IDEA FOR YOU...

Earnings management is not only done to make the figures better than they really are. Sometimes the firm wants to make them look a bit worse! For instance, to hide fantastically good profits from hostile eyes. Suppose you are a pharmaceutical company that is making an incredible fortune in Ruritania; you don't really want the Ruritanians to know how well you are doing, or they'll start passing laws to take away your profits. Such companies may actually be a bargain.

42 LOOKING FOR BARGAINS

'Give yourself a real good mark if you know that a business should make money, but only if you really know it.'

As well as finding a good business, we want to find one whose share price makes it a bargain. So how do we go about doing this? One way is to look at a company's price to book ratios.

The price to book ratio is the price per share/ book value of equity per share. The book value is the total assets of the company minus its liabilities. Book value tends to be a relatively stable number, and is useful for comparisons between firms operating under similar accounting rules. Remember though, that some countries let firms state a relatively high book value, so you will have to make adjustments for this, and that some industries, such as high technology, may not have many tangible assets.

DEFINING IDEA...

(An investor) should be able to justify every purchase he makes and each price he pays by impersonal, objective reasoning.

– BENJAMIN GRAHAM, VALUE INVESTOR

Quite a few studies have found a strong link between low price/book ratios and above average returns. If this continues in the future, the rewards of investing in such 'bargains' should be reasonably good. The famous value investor, Benjamin Graham, who died in the 1950s, always looked for low price/book ratios as one of the most important criteria for investment. However, his ceiling was very stringent; he was only interested in companies whose share price was less than two thirds of book value. Companies like this tend not to be growing – Graham's attitude was that they were 'like cigar butts with one or two good puffs left in them'.

Another useful measure, this time for analysing firms that are expected to grow fast, is the price/equity to growth (PEG) ratio. This is calculated as the price earnings ratio (P/E) / the expected growth rate per share. If the PEG ratio is low, the firm is considered a potential 'buy' when compared with other firms that have similar dividend rates, risk levels and expected growth. When you calculate the P/E, you must make sure that it matches the earning period that you are using.

A third useful ratio is the price/sales ratio. This is the market value of equity/ annual sales. Some analysts like this ratio because it removes several possible biases. For example, many companies calculate their book value and earnings per share differently, which makes them hard to compare with one another. The price/sales ratio, on the other hand, deals with 'real' sales figures and makes the figures easier to compare. The companies that are most likely to be undervalued on this measure are those with a low price/sales ratio and high profit margins.

HERE'S AN IDEA FOR YOU...

Ratios are really useful ways of comparing the relative merits of companies. When using them, you should always check that: you define the ratio clearly; you apply it in the same way to all the companies; you know what ratio values are typical for the industry you are looking at; and that you are comparing companies that are similar. Remember, also, that the results you get are only educated guesses – they are not absolute facts – and you should only use them to get a 'feel' for the nature of the firms.

43 DISCOUNTED CASH FLOW

'The more financial predictions you make the more business you do and the more commissions you get.'

DEFINING IDEA...

I don't want a lot of good investments; I want a few outstanding ones.

– PHILIP FISHER, GROWTH INVESTOR

Discounted Cash Flow (DCF) is based on the idea that the value of anything, whether an asset or a company, is the sum total of the cash it can generate in the future, adjusted for the present value of that cash. DCF analyses a company in detail from the bottom up, unlike the ratios we looked at in the previous chapter, which analyse from the top down. The aim is to obtain a more accurate estimate of value, which it may actually do, depending on the skill and judgement of the analyst.

DCF can be defined as the total sum of all the residual cash flows (that's the cash left over after all expenses, including reinvestment), adjusted for their value in today's money. The reason why you have to adjust them for today's money (which is called 'present value') is easy to understand from the following example. Your friend borrows £100 from you at no interest and offers you two choices: he'll either pay it back tomorrow or in 5 years' time. Presumably you would prefer to have the money tomorrow. To calculate the value of the money coming in five years' time, you have to 'discount' it. This is done with the formula: present value = number of years until the money is paid / (1 + interest rate)n = number of years.

There are lots of ways to calculate DCF, some of them fiendishly complicated. To get the general idea, let's look at an easy example, such as a very stable company with predictable growth and a steady record of dividend payments. The formula, known as the dividend discount model, is: the fair share price = next year's dividend / (required rate of return – expected dividend growth rate). Supposing the company pays a dividend of $2, that investors can obtain a 'risk-free' return of 8% from bonds and that dividends are expected to grow by 5% annually, and we set the required rate of return at 10%, a little higher than the bond rate, the 'correct' value of the share price would be: $2 / (0.1 – 0.05) = $40. If the current share price is less than $40 dollars, then the company is a bargain, according to these figures.

From the investor's point of view, the only cash flow that will ever be received is from dividends (and the sale of the shares). The dividend discount model is supposed to give long term investors, who aren't going to sell their shares, a realistic valuation. People often complain that it produces figures that are too conservative, but studies have shown that the model works quite well in identifying firms that are bargains, subject to all sorts of qualifications (for example, it only really works for stable companies).

HERE'S AN IDEA FOR YOU...

Like most of the complicated sums financial analysts do, DCF can be misused to give the impression of precision where this is impossible – like all estimates, it is based on assumptions. But it's worth learning how to do, because it makes you really get inside the realities of a company's business.

44 STOCK MARKET NEWSLETTERS

'Some statisticians have to write weekly, and even daily, 'market letters'. This is a tough way to make a living. It not only requires the constant making of predictions, but it requires putting the predictions down on paper for anyone interested to check up on ... Statisticians of a nervous, sensitive sort ... develop a prose style which would make a German nineteenth century metaphysician envious.'

DEFINING IDEA...
Never ask a barber if you need a haircut.
~ WARREN BUFFETT

In Schwed's day people who studied shares professionally were called 'statisticians'; now they are called 'financial analysts', and the really famous ones become 'gurus'. Then, as now, some of them were on the 'buy' side, telling their employers what to buy and sell, while others were on the 'sell' side, telling customers what they should do. Most of the analysts you will encounter as an investor will be on the sell side.

Therein lies the problem. Customers want to buy, and sell side analysts want to tell them what to buy. Some customers are suspicious of institutional advice, so they go to independent suppliers of analysis. There are lots of independent sources of information you can subscribe to, ranging from very populist and low grade stock market newsletters to highly sophisticated specialist ones that concentrate on very specific areas. You can also follow columnists' share picks in the financial pages of the national press.

Whatever source of analysis you use, the basic problem is the same. You, the investing public, have an insatiable appetite for buy and sell recommendations. And all these services exist to satisfy this demand. Often there is nothing to say, but the analysts still have to write something or the pages of their newsletters would be blank. So the writers have to resort to all sorts of stratagems to say something interesting.

One way to do this is to make some kind of extreme prediction – either positive or negative – that will make people sit up and think. 'The US market will quadruple within three years.' 'No hope for shares in our lifetime.' As long as it grabs the reader's attention, it doesn't matter that it's garbage. The trouble is, you probably have to stick to your line for the rest of your career (some stock market gurus really do this!), which can become tiresome. Keep on repeating the prediction, with slight variations, and one day you will be right. Try to make a lot of money by writing books and appearing on TV at that point.

Another method, the one that Schwed mentions, is followed by people who have to make predictions but don't like to be wrong. This is tricky, but it can be done by writing in a vague, ambiguous but technical sounding way about movements in the market. Ideally your pieces should be capable of being interpreted in many different ways. Then, at least, nobody can accuse you of being wrong.

HERE'S AN IDEA FOR YOU...

An interesting recent survey investigated whether there was any link between the accuracy of stockmarket gurus' predictions and the amount of attention they get on the internet. The researchers found absolutely no correlation. That could mean that people just use gurus to stimulate their ideas, and not for their predictions. That is a sensible approach.

45 LIFE PLAN

'I have actually been fiddling around with common stocks for most of my life.'

When you go to a financial adviser these days, the first thing she has to do is to conduct a fact find; this is required by the regulators. It's a good rule, because you have to look at your life in the round – your income, your prospects, your liabilities, your dependents – to make a sensible plan.

DEFINING IDEA...

Always be a first-rate version of yourself, instead of a second-rate version of somebody else.

– JUDY GARLAND

One approach to this is to think about your life as a series of stages, with different needs and opportunities occurring at different times. Although the retail end of the financial services industry makes this into a rather irritating, paternalistic 'we know better than you do' ploy, the basic idea is sound – you just have to tailor it to suit who you are, not who the bank thinks you ought to be.

Most people don't plan enough for the medium to long term, as many studies have established. A very effective technique for ensuring that you are in control of your finances is to set aside money for specific purposes. Suppose you know that within five years you will need to renovate your kitchen. By regularly paying money into a separate account, you can ensure that you will have the cash when the time comes.

Using this technique, you can then think about your stages of life more clearly. Let's divide them into four: young adulthood, building a family, middle age and retirement.

Young adulthood: people in their twenties naturally have a big appetite for life but usually are earning less than they will later on. Many people at this stage tend to spend too easily. There is a danger of getting into debt. On the other hand, any sound long term investment is likely to grow substantially. Try contributing a small sum each month to an index fund.

Building a family: if you are starting a family, your expenditure is likely to have increased dramatically. Purchasing a home is an important form of long term saving. You also need to start planning for retirement.

Middle age: by this time many people have got some equity in their homes and are at the top of their career and earning power. Now is the time to put as much money as possible into your investments and pension scheme, if you have one.

Retirement: if you don't have to retire, then don't! But if you do, this is when you may have to live off your investments. Protecting your capital becomes very important, so many people start to weight their portfolios heavily towards bonds, which have a predictable return if held to maturity.

HERE'S AN IDEA FOR YOU...

Take a two–pronged approach: first, save for specific medium term goals, like new kitchens, keeping the money in a separate fund; second, contribute to a general, long term stock market fund to build up financial assets for the future. Be cautious about schemes that tie you up forever; although some pension schemes are still generous and worthwhile, many of us are going to have to save for ourselves, so the sooner you start, the better.

46 HEDGE FUNDS

'[Hedging] supplies the speculator with definite insurance, 'term insurance', actually. But like all insurance it costs money to buy. Thus the simple question is set: is the price of the insurance commensurate with the amount of the protection gained?'

Hedge funds are a specialised type of professionally managed portfolio that are much less heavily regulated than other kinds of collective investment, and are also much less transparent. Many of them use derivatives extensively in the pursuit of high returns.

DEFINING IDEA...
(Hedge funds are) Wall Street's Pied Pipers of Performance.
– WARREN BUFFETT

To call most of these funds 'hedge' is misleading, because most of them do not hedge as their main activity. To 'hedge' means to reduce risk by buying a new risk to cancel out an existing risk. In a perfect world the two risks would cancel each other out perfectly, but in reality most hedges don't do this; this means that there is an extra risk that both positions go wrong, resulting in an even bigger loss.

Hedging isn't confined to hedge funds. Most professional investors hedge sometimes. Let's say you are worried that the FTSE 100 is going to fall next year, but you don't want to sell your shares. You can sell an index future short, or buy a 'put' (the right to sell at a pre-agreed price) on an index to protect against a decline in the value of the shares you hold. You can hedge against the risk that interest rates will fall, or that an exchange rate will go against you, or any number of a whole host of possible risks, and you don't need a hedge fund to do it.

Many hedge funds have medium-high to very-high risk approaches. They generally seek to make above-average returns by using very complex strategies. Sometimes this involves some genuine hedging, but often they assume high risks of other kinds, in pursuit of their ambitious investment objectives. At the really high risk end, they go in for 'macro-management' – the fund managers seek to exploit changes in value caused by political and economic events. Some managers are willing to take positions in virtually any security or market in the world, often with very heavy leverage. George Soros, the professional investor well-known for his high profile currency speculation, is a 'macro-manager'. Other fairly risky strategies include looking for special situations such as mergers and acquisitions. The fund may do things like buying shares in the target company while simultaneously short-selling the stock of the acquiring company, and using gearing (i.e. borrowed money) to increase the potential gain or loss.

If the foregoing hasn't put you off already, and you are interested in investing in a hedge fund, you should examine its strategy very closely. Hedge funds often require you to 'lock-up' your investment for a period and may not open for transactions on a daily basis. In general you should expect to hold a hedge fund investment for at least three years.

HERE'S AN IDEA FOR YOU...

Hedge funds haven't been performing well lately, so by the time you read this they may be a thing of the past. In my opinion, they are best avoided, at least in their present form, because you really don't know how risky they are – and most of them are much, much more risky than boring old unit trusts and investment trusts.

47 SOME IMPORTANT BASICS

'It should not be too radical to suggest that a young man entering [Wall] Street should have some special mental equipment beyond one complete set of smoking-room stories about Mr. and Mrs. Roosevelt.'

The effect of compound interest is the principal reason why long term investments perform better than short-term investments. It's a simple mathematical process that produces amazing results. The secret of successful investing is patience. The longer you hold an investment, the more it is likely to grow, simply through the effect of compound interest.

DEFINING IDEA...

The most powerful force in the universe is compound interest.

~ ALBERT EINSTEIN

For example if you invest £100 at a modest real (inflation adjusted) rate of return of 5%, after one year you will have £105. After that, though, you will start getting interest on the interest. In the early years that figure is small. In the later years, however, it starts to grow like a snowball without you having to add any further cash to the investment (as long as you reinvest your dividends). After 5 years, the sum will have grown to £128, after 10 years to £163, after 20 years to £265 and after 25 years to £339. The situation is even beter if you can get a real rate of return of 7%, which is about the highest return you can realistically aim at from the stock market without taking excessive risk: after 5 years, the sum will have grown to £140, after 10 years to £197, after 20 years to £387 and after 25 years to £543.

A useful way to estimate how long it will take an investment to double at a given rate of interest is 'the rule of 72'. Simply divide the annual interest rate into 72, and you will get the approximate length of time it will take to double. For example, how long does it take for £100 to double at a return of 5%? 72/5 = 14.4, so it will take about 14.4 years.

Since a small increase in the rate of return will make a huge difference to the growth of your investment over the long term, it is important to minimise investment charges because they can substantially reduce your overall return in later years.

Let's not forget inflation. Always try to do your calculations based on an estimate of the 'inflation-adjusted', or 'real', rate of return, which is simply the return in money minus the rate of inflation. Whenever you look at figures for investment performance, always check whether they are inflation-adjusted. You might be surprised at how many are not inflation-adjusted.

Also, you don't know what the inflation rates will be in the future, so you will have to keep your eye on them when judging how your investments are performing. Here's an amazing fact: between 1700 and 1900 UK prices went up by more than 6,000%!

HERE'S AN IDEA FOR YOU...

Don't forget the possibility that deflationary periods can occur, although they are rare. This is when there is a general fall in prices. 'Cash is king' during deflationary periods because you can purchase valuable assets at bargain prices – but you may have to wait a long time before you can sell these assets for a profit.

48 BEHAVIOURAL FINANCE

'It is the belief of the management of this corporation that a diversified list of carefully selected securities, held over a period of time, will not increase in value.'

DEFINING IDEA...

Extremely few companies have been able to show a high rate of uninterrupted growth for long periods of time.

~ BENJAMIN GRAHAM,
THE FATHER OF SECURITY ANALYSIS

Traditionally the theoretical study of the stock market assumed that investors were pretty rational people, and tried to explain stock market phenomena in terms of rational behaviour. The problem with this is that a lot of people, even sensible people, don't behave rationally all the time, and some people don't seem to behave rationally any of the time. Recognising this, in recent years some boffins have been trying to explain what might be going on – it's called 'behavioural finance'.

In Fred Schwed's quote above, he's making a point about really talented investors, in this case a young fund manager called John Pope who made a fortune between the Wall Street Crash of 1929 and his untimely death in 1931, during the early years of the Depression. The point is that Pope concentrated his investments in positions he was sure about, and didn't worry about diversification. He sold a lot of troubled shares short, and got a lot of flak for it but, as history was to show, the 1930s got a lot worse before they got better.

Companies listed on the stock markets have widely varying returns, so at any point in time there will always be a few companies producing extraordinarily good returns and a few with extraordinarily bad returns. To some extent, this effect is random, in the same way as the outcome of tossing a coin is random. Top-performing mutual funds, for example, tend not to stay at the top for very long – if they have a very good result in one year, they may have only an average result in the following year.

This effect is called 'regression to the mean', which simply means that over time results will tend towards the long term historical average. That's why measurements of the average overall performance of a stock market, such as indices (see chapter 13), are important. It is probable that, over time, a mutual fund will tend to produce results in line with the long term average performance of the types of investment it makes. It is not probable that a mutual fund will go on and on outperforming similar funds of its type for many years.

HERE'S AN IDEA FOR YOU...

The phenomenon of regression to the mean suggests that over the very long term the outstanding investment portfolios will wind up doing about the same as the averages, as measured by indices. That seems to be happening to Warren Buffett's portfolio, as he is the first to admit. As his fund has grown bigger and bigger, he finds it harder and harder to find winning investments that will make a significant difference to his bottom line – they're all too small! This suggests two things – first, the value of index investing over the long term, and second, that you may find bigger profit opportunities among the smaller companies, rather than the bigger ones.

49 BUSINESS IS HARD

'Our society suffers dreadfully from the fact that there are so few of us who, in ourselves, have services or talents that we can sell for as much as a hundred dollars a week.'

What Fred Schwed means here is that a lot of people go into business, or try to make a business out of investing, because they don't have anything better to do. When you are really good at something, he is saying, then you don't need to do this if you can make an excellent income from your talent, whether it is being a good salesperson or an expert animal trainer.

DEFINING IDEA...

Failures don't plan to fail, they fail to plan.

– HARVEY MACKAY, BUSINESSMAN

It is the same with business. You can do well if you are good at it, but the reality is that most people aren't. Every year, whether times are good or bad, thousands of enterprises, mainly small firms, go bust in the UK – that's about 5% of all businesses, each year . The average life expectancy for a start up business is two years. Currently, the businesses most likely to fail are courier and haulage companies (it must be the oil prices), and restaurants and bars (are people going out less?). Twenty years ago it was clothes boutiques and small builders. You might think that this is because of the UK's amazingly hostile environment to new businesses, but that's not the whole story. The US, for instance, is a lot more business friendly, but over 70% of start ups are finished within the first year, and 90% don't last 10 years.

Those are terrible odds! How can it be? The three main reasons are generally thought to be: choosing an unprofitable business, not having enough capital to run the business, and generally inadequate management. That all boils down to one thing – you, the person who starts the business. Starting a business is not a good way of finding a way of making a living if you happen to lose your job, for instance. You'll find yourself working a lot longer hours for a lot less money, at least in the early years. And statistically speaking, the early years are the only ones you are likely to get.

Some people think that trading in the stock market could be a good way of making a living. You just make a few good trades every month, maybe on the options market, and the rest of your time will be free. Not so! The odds are overwhelmingly against you, and it's an even worse way to try to make a living than opening a cocktail bar.

Neither running a business nor frequent trading are good ways for getting income that you lack, unless you are especially able. Work on what you're good at, get more training, and get a real job.

HERE'S AN IDEA FOR YOU...

Still determined to start a business? Good for you, maybe. You may have the energy and determination that it takes to succeed. Here's an idea that most entrepreneurs learn the hard way: don't start a business, buy one that is already running. You're much more likely to make a go of something that is a going concern. And remember, be a tough investor, and don't pay too much for it.

50 LOSS

'Like all of life's rich emotional experiences, the full flavour of losing important money cannot be conveyed in literature.'

DEFINING IDEA...

Nothing stings us so bitterly as the loss of money.

- LIVY, ROMAN HISTORIAN

Most human beings, it seems, are not born with an ability to perceive risks objectively. Suppose you are planning to go on holiday in a foreign country and you hear news reports of an attack on tourists in the south of the country, hundreds of miles from where you are going. Should you cancel your trip?

Many people would cancel, even if there is no real danger. The reason is that we tend to give too much weight to very dramatic scare stories when we have only recently heard them (the effect wears off over time). If we hear wild news reports of an economic crisis and an impending stock market crash, we may want to sell all our equities at a rock-bottom price, even if the chances of an eventual recovery are good. The lesson? Don't overreact to frightening news – it may not be as bad as it seems.

Another form of being afraid to lose happens when there is a big competition to buy something, as in an auction. Often, the successful purchaser is likely to pay too much. You see this happening in the stock market all the time. Some investment fad becomes huge, everybody hears about it and starts feeling that they are idiots for not piling in. Businesses often do it too. For example, during the 1990s, when telecommunications companies vastly overpaid for government licences for mobile communications networks in the US, Europe and elsewhere. Then the big story was that acquiring more 'bandwidth' was a sure way to success, but now, years later, many bandwidth owners have been unable even to recover their costs.

The more bidders there are for something, the more they are likely to overpay, according to research. Seeing many other eager buyers appears to give a bidder more confidence that the item is valuable. You often see investment crazes in the stock market, and people who really ought to know better get caught up in them. One of the first big crazes was in 1720 in England, when speculation in a firm, the South Sea Company, caused a serious financial crisis known as the South Sea Bubble. The South Sea Company was a fairly unprofitable outfit that transported slaves from Africa to the Americas, but through some creative financing (including the bribery of senior members of the government) it sparked a wild boom in its shares, which went from about £100 in 1719 to £1,000 in August 1720. You could buy the shares in instalments (i.e. you didn't have to pay for them all at once), and August 1720 was when the first instalment became due. You can probably guess the rest – the shares were down to £150 by the following month, and many people lost everything they had, because they had borrowed so much to buy the shares at a high price.

HERE'S AN IDEA FOR YOU...

Whenever you invest, always think about the possibility that you might lose all your money, and how that might happen. Then do something to limit your loss. That might mean investing less, or it might mean spreading the cash across different, but similar vehicles, like having several savings accounts in different banks.

51 THE 'FAT, STUPID PEASANT' APPROACH

'[After selling shares at a profit] … a long time later it turns out that I should have just bought them, and thereafter sat on them like a fat, stupid peasant. A peasant, however, who is rich beyond his limited dreams of avarice.'

DEFINING IDEA...

Time is your friend; impulse is your enemy.

– JOHN BOGLE, FAMOUS INVESTOR

In this book we have identified two promising routes to a making a good return in the stock market: index investing and buying companies with good fundamentals at a time when their share prices are low. The first is extremely easy to do, and although it can never perform better than the index that it follows, that really shouldn't matter very much, since it will still probably produce a better return than investing in any other type of financial security over the long term. We say 'probably' because nothing in life is certain, and even indices can potentially become highly volatile, if too much money starts sloshing in and out of index funds, for instance.

The second approach is rather more difficult because it is much harder to establish any objective view of what good fundamentals might actually mean. Warren Buffett is certain he knows what he means by it, and has been extraordinarily successful at investing, but that doesn't mean we can be successful by trying to copy him. Also, lots of other people have strong ideas about what good fundamentals are and have been much less successful at investment.

What both approaches have in common is that both require an investment for the long term. For your whole life, in fact. Part of the reason for this is the effect of compounding (see chapter 47). If you just keep on holding, reinvesting the dividends (and the company keeps on reinvesting the rest of its profits to create growth), the longer you hold your shares the better. You may think that the glory days of the American economy are over or that Britain is going to the dogs, but overall, when you look at the whole world, with its young, eager population that is willing to work and willing to consume, do you really think that the processes of modernisation and increasing productivity are going to decline? There are, surely, good grounds for moderate optimism, and by investing in the stock market you should be able to become a beneficiary of worldwide growth. As long as the UK and US markets remain important players on the world stage you can invest through them in the rest of the world, if that is your preference, and if the day ever comes when, say, Shanghai and São Paulo become the world's centres of finance, you should get enough warning to be able to make the shift.

This, in my opinion at least, is a good argument for patient, long term investing – what you might call the 'fat, stupid peasant' approach.

HERE'S AN IDEA FOR YOU

One way of looking at the difference between index investing and selecting outstanding companies is to say that the first is a passive method and that the second is active. In other words, the second is more risky, takes a lot more effort and time, and may depend on your intellectual ability. But in any case, don't forget to add to your stock market portfolio by saving out of your income; over the years, this can build up to a very tidy sum.

52 BOOKS ON THE STOCK MARKET

'Books about Wall Street fall into two categories which may respectively be called the admiring "Oh, My!" School and the vindictive, or "Throw the Rascals Out" School.'

DEFINING IDEA...

Investors have very short memories.

~ ROMAN ABRAMOVICH, RUSSIAN BILLIONAIRE

Every year hundreds of books about the stock market are published – more during bull markets than bear markets, naturally. They aren't all useless; many of them provide up-to-date information on new investment situations and new investment techniques that are constantly developing. There are always new things to say, of a technical nature, about the oil business, say, or derivatives, or changes in taxation. These kinds of books form a separate category, what one might call the 'Useful' School.

Fred Schwed's two categories mainly apply to popular books. The 'Oh, My!' School is typified by come-on titles, like *Day Trade Your Way Out of Debt!* (a spoof title). Mostly published in the US, these books are aimed at readers who want to make a lot of money quickly. The only way to do this , of course, is to take a lot of risk, which means that your chances of success are actually quite small. The books tend to focus on schemes that use Technical Analysis (see chapter 16), frequent trading (see chapter 31) and speculating with borrowed money (which is never a good idea). Nevertheless, they can be quite useful as introductions to the very wide range of investment approaches out there. For example, there are lots of admiring books about Warren Buffett, who, in my opinion, really is one of the greatest investors of all time, and such books do supply useful material about his methods.

The 'Throw the Rascals Out' School isn't totally useless either. Every scandal, fraud, bankruptcy and financial crisis generates a slew of volumes to explain what happened. I'm eagerly waiting for some to come out about Bernie Madoff (see chapter 32) at the moment. A lot of them are pretty hysterical, though. The silliest ones are those that predict the imminent total collapse of the world as we know it. These may provide some cheap thrills to people who like fiction about dystopias, but they aren't to be taken seriously. Of course it is true that the modern financial system is unstable (most theorists believe that it can't be otherwise), and we have plenty of examples from the past of hard times occurring, but it is surely better to actively pursue financial security than to passively sit and wait for an apocalypse that may never come.

The most important thing, though, is to read a good range of books, because this will give you a sense of how old most of the arguments are, and how the same things keep happening in the markets again and again. Doing this will inoculate you against doing anything rash.

HERE'S AN IDEA FOR YOU...

By all means build up a library of new investment books, but don't neglect the classics – they will provide you with a solid foundation of investment theories and techniques that have stood the test of time. Some of the classics are a bit stodgy, like Benjamin Graham's The Intelligent Investor, *and some a bit eccentric, like Philip Fisher's* Common Stocks, Uncommon Profits, *but they are definitely worth the effort of wading through them.*

INDEX

Note: page numbers in bold indicate *Defining ideas*
or *Here's an idea* for you sections.

Made in the USA
Middletown, DE
09 March 2015